WHERE DO WE GO FROM HERE

April 4, 1968: Rev. Martin Luther King, Jr., just prior to making his final public appearance to address striking Memphis sanitation workers. King was assassinated later that day outside his motel room. (AP/Wide World Photos)

WHERE DO WE GO FROM HERE

Chaos or Community?

MARTIN LUTHER KING, JR.

BEACON PRESS

BOSTON

BEACON PRESS
25 Beacon Street
Boston, Massachusetts 02108-2892

Beacon Press books are published under the auspices of
the Unitarian Universalist Association of Congregations.

—THE—
KING In Association With **IPM**
LEGACY INTELLECTUAL PROPERTIES
MANAGEMENT, INC.

This edition of *Where Do We Go from Here* is based on the 1967 edition
published in the United States by Harper & Row Publishers, Inc.
Some spelling and punctuation have been adjusted,
and obvious errors have been corrected.

Printed in the United States of America

13 12 11 10   8 7 6 5 4 3 2 1

Composition by Wilsted & Taylor Publishing Services

Library of Congress Cataloging-in-Publication Data can be found on page 226.

*To the committed supporters of the civil rights
movement, Negro and white, whose steadfastness amid
confusions and setbacks gives assurance that brotherhood will
be the condition of man, not the dream of man*

*A special note of thanks is due Hermine I. Popper,
whose editorial skills and warm spirit of cooperation
contributed greatly toward the completion of this book.*

CONTENTS

Introduction by Vincent Harding *ix*

Foreword by Coretta Scott King *xxiii*

I

Where Are We? *1*

II

Black Power *23*

III

Racism and the White Backlash *71*

IV

The Dilemma of Negro Americans *109*

V

Where We Are Going *143*

VI

The World House *177*

Appendix: Programs and Prospects *203*

Notes *215*

Index *217*

INTRODUCTION

Having shared a precious friendship with Martin King during the last ten years of his life, I was very pleased to learn that Beacon Press was returning to its important role as a publisher of his book-length works. Then, when I was asked to write the introduction for this new edition of King's fourth book, many powerful memories flooded my being. First and most important was my recollection of how determined Martin was to be fully and creatively engaged with the living history of his time, a history he did so much to help create but also a dangerous and tumultuous history that shaped and transformed his own amazingly brief yet momentous searching life.

From this position of radical engagement it would have been relatively easy for King, if he chose, to confine his published writing to telling the powerful stories of the experiences he shared almost daily with the magnificent band of women, men, and children who worked in the black-led Southern freedom movement, recounting how they struggled to transform themselves, their communities, this nation, and our world. Instead, going beyond the stories, King insisted on constantly raising and reflecting on the basic questions he posed in the first chapter of this work—"Where Are

We?" and in the overall title of the book itself, *Where Do We Go from Here: Chaos or Community?* (Always present, of course, were the deepest questions of all: Who are we? Who are we meant to be?)

These are the recognizable queries that mature human beings persistently pose to themselves—and to their communities—as they explore the way toward their best possibilities. Not surprisingly, such constant probing toward self-understanding was a central element of King's practice when he was at his best.

Indeed, it was the urgent need for such self-examination and deep reflection on the new American world that he and the freedom movement helped create that literally drove King to wrestle publicly and boldly with the profound issues of this book. Ironically, it was almost immediately after the extraordinary success of the heroic Alabama voter-registration campaign—which led to the Selma-to-Montgomery march, and the follow-up congressional passage of the 1965 Voting Rights Act—that King realized he had to confront a very difficult set of emerging American realities that demanded his best prophetic interpretation and his most creative proposals for action.

Perhaps the most immediate and symbolic energizing event came just days after President Lyndon Johnson signed the hard-won historic Voting Rights Act, when the black community of Watts, in Los Angeles, exploded in fire, frustration, and rage. When King and several of his coworkers rushed to Watts to engage some of the young men who were most deeply involved in the uprising, they heard the youth say, "We won." Looking at the still smoldering embers of the local community, the visitors asked what *winning* meant, and one of the young men declared, "We won because we made them pay attention to us."

Building on all of the deep resources of empathy and compassion that seemed so richly and naturally a part of his life, King appeared determined not only to pay attention but to insist that his organization and his nation focus themselves and their resources on dozens of poor, exploited black communities—and especially their desperate young men, whose broken lives were crying out for new, humane possibilities in the midst of the wealthiest nation in the world. Speaking later at a staff retreat of the Southern Christian Leadership Conference, King expressed a conviction that had long been a crucial part of what he saw when he paid attention to the nation's poorest people. He said, "Something is wrong with the economic system of our nation. . . . Something is wrong with capitalism." Always careful (perhaps too careful) to announce that he was not a Marxist in any sense of the word, King told the staff he believed "there must be a better distribution of wealth, and maybe America must move toward a democratic socialism. . . . " This seemed a natural direction for someone whose ultimate societal goal was the achievement of a nonviolent "beloved community." But a major part of the white American community and its mass media seemed only able to condemn "Negro violence" and to justify a "white backlash" against the continuing attempts of the freedom movement to move northward toward a more perfect union. (King wisely indentified the fashionable "backlash" as a continuing expression of an antidemocratic white racism that was as old as the nation itself.)

Meanwhile, even before Watts, King and the SCLC staff had begun to explore creative ways in which they could expand their effort to develop a just and beloved national community by establishing projects in northern black urban neighborhoods. (The Student Nonviolent Coordinating Committee, or SNCC, the other major Southern movement organizing force, was involved in similar Northern explorations by the mid-1960s, but both organizations were hampered by severe financial difficulties.) Partly because of some earlier contacts with Chicago-based community organizers, King and SCLC decided to focus on that deeply segregated city as the center of their expansion into the anguish of the North. By the winter of 1966, SCLC staff members had begun organizing in Chicago. At that point King decided to try to spend at least three days a week actually living in one of the city's poorest black communities, a west-side area named Lawndale. From that vantage point, working (sometimes uncomfortably) with their Chicago colleagues, King and SCLC decided to concentrate their attention on a continuing struggle against the segregated, deteriorating, and educationally dysfunctional schools; the often dilapidated housing; and the disheartening lack of job opportunities.

This book must be read in the urgent context of King's difficult experiences in Watts and Chicago, which seemed more representative of the nation's deeper racial dilemma than were the Southern battlegrounds of Selma and Montgomery. For instance, Chicago was the setting for King's fierce reminders that "the economic plight of the masses of Negroes has worsened" since the beginnings of the Southern freedom movement, because slum conditions had worsened "and Negroes attend more thoroughly segregated schools than in 1954."

In the face of such hard facts, King insisted on pressing two other realities into the nation's conscience. One was his continuing plea for "a coalition of Negroes and liberal whites that will work to make both major parties truly responsive to the needs of the poor." At the same time he insisted that "we must not be oblivious to the fact that the larger economic problems confronting the Negro community will only be solved by federal programs involving billions of dollars."

This was the King of *Where Do We Go from Here*. Sparked by the young men of Watts, informed by the streets he walked in Chicago, inspired by the magnificently ordinary organizers and community members who faced white rage and fear-filled violence in the Windy City and its suburbs, King was constantly teaching, learning, urging, admonishing—reminding Americans not only of the powerful obstacles in our histories, our institutions, and our hearts, but also calling our attention to the amazing hope represented by Thomas Paine, one of the few really radical, grassroots-oriented "founding fathers," who dared to proclaim, "We have the power to begin the world over again." Insisting on claiming such revolutionary words, King readily grasped them for himself and for us all. Mixing all this with his undying commitment to the way of active nonviolence, King remained faithful to the call he had put forth at the end of the Selma-to-Montgomery march: "We must keep going." (Always going, always carrying the costly testimony: "Occasionally in life one develops a conviction so precious and meaningful that he will stand on it till the end. That is what I have found in nonviolence.")

Ironically enough, while King's time in Chicago placed its indelible mark on both his questions and his relentless search for answers—for himself and for the rest of us—it was another Southern-based experience that pressed him to share some of his deepest convictions, hopes, and fears. Indeed, the recounting of his crucial participation in the June 1966 Mississippi March Against Fear (the "Meredith March") provided King the opportunity he needed to offer some of his own powerful responses to the fear-tinged, media-driven national debate about the rise and meaning of the call for Black Power and the spread of the urban black explosions inadequately called "riots."

In addition to offering his own constantly expanding appreciation of the positive, healing elements of a black self-love, King continued to urge the African American community to refuse to let the path toward black affirmation lead into the self-defeating way of isolation and despair. "There is no solution for the Negro through isolation," he wrote. Instead, encouraging black people to continue moving on toward our best possibilities (instead of copying white America's worst habits—especially its racism, extreme materialism, and militarism), King declared that "our most fruitful course is to stand firm, move forward nonviolently, accept disappointment and cling to hope." In that same frame of mind, King added, "To guard ourselves from bitterness we need the vision to see in this generation's ordeals the opportunity to transfigure both ourselves and American society." (Did he foresee the Obama opportunity? Will Obama really see King, paying attention? And what about us? Where do we go? The questions cannot be avoided.)

At the same time, King took the opportunity to speak to white allies whose support for the freedom movement had already diminished as the campaign moved on to address the harsh realities and structural challenges of the North. In that context, King called Black Power a cry of "disappointment with timid white moderates who feel that they can set the timetable for the Negro's freedom." With increasing regularity, that theme of black disappointment (that he surely shared) was also applied to the Johnson administration and its devastating war in Vietnam. Indeed, as the war expanded, drawing more and more American troops (mostly poor, working class, and people of color on the front lines), as it endangered and destroyed the lives of hundreds of thousands of Vietnamese people, King's protesting, conscience-driven voice began to be heard with increasing vigor. And *Where Do We Go from Here* provided another opportunity to contrast the comparative timidity and lack of creativity of Johnson's cut-rate War on Poverty to the robust energy, imagination and billons of dollars dedicated to the Southeast Asian disaster. That was the setting in which King described the call for Black Power as an urgent scream of "disappointment with a federal administration that seems to be more concerned about winning an ill-considered war in Vietnam than about winning the war against poverty here at home."

Even as he spoke and wrote those words, King recognized the danger they carried. He knew that there were many black and white allies and supporters of his organization and of the larger freedom and justice movement who considered it unwise, unpatriotic, and unnecessarily provocative to combine the call for legal and economic rights at home with a profound questioning of the foreign policy of a federal government whose assistance was considered essential in the achievement of civil rights. (King knew as well that many of his sturdy financial contributors were having difficulty continuing to give support toward such unorthodox views—especially when they tended to expect black people to be superpatriots, in the most narrow definition of the word. And, of course, King also knew that Lyndon Johnson expected nothing less than utter fealty, in gratitude for his role as the "Civil Rights president.")

Interestingly enough, in the course of his insistent wrestling with the purpose and future direction of his own organization and of the larger movement, King used the pages of this book to press himself and his coworkers to move beyond a narrow, legalistic understanding of their work, to

open themselves to newer, deeper, less-travelled directions—
especially as they faced the systemic, social, political, and
economic issues that met them everywhere in the North.

For instance, toward the end of this work, as King envi-
sioned for himself and others some aspects of a human response to the book's title question, he wrote, "So far we
have had constitutional backing for most of our demands for
change, and this has made our work easier, since we could
be sure of legal support from the federal courts. Now we are
approaching areas where the voice of the Constitution is not
clear." King went on with his description of the new situation, saying, "We have left the realm of constitutional rights
and we are entering the area of human rights." He continued: "The Constitution assured the right to vote, but there
is no such assurance of the right to adequate housing, or the
right to an adequate income. [Or, the right to high-quality
education and health care?] And yet in a nation which has
a gross national product of $750 billion a year, it is morally
right to insist that every person have a decent house, an adequate education and enough money to provide basic necessities for one's family." Here again he urged exploration of a
"guaranteed annual income" for all who needed it.

For the many persons—whatever their color—who originally signed onto the freedom movement to assist in the quest
for the Southern black right to vote, for equal access to public accommodations, and for minimally integrated schools,
this King was out beyond their vision and their reach—and
their control. For me, as I revisit *this* King and remember his
last years of unrelenting struggle against what he called "the
triple evils" of racism, materialism, and militarism, I see him
on the nettlesome, uncharted path toward a more perfect
union, a path that still challenges us all. I hear him preaching
at his Ebenezer Church in Atlanta: "I choose to identify with

the underprivileged. I choose to identify with the poor. I choose to give my life for the hungry. . . . This is the way I'm going. If it means suffering a little bit, I'm going that way. If it means sacrificing, I'm going that way. If it means dying for them, I'm going that way, because I heard a voice say, 'Do something for others.' "

And I rejoice to consider the strong possibility that *this* King, while paying attention, had opened the way for Barack Obama. So I pray and work that the best of King and the best of Obama might meet, both enriched, both made vulnerable and powerful by their attention to the cries of Chicago's poorest people, both opening to all of us the opportunity to stand with them—again and again, pressing them and ourselves to respond to our best angels.

Throughout this book, King continues to combine his various roles—as spirit-based, pro-democracy activist; thoughtful social analyst; loving, encouraging pastor who calls us to our best possibilities; and as justice-obsessed, biblically shaped, prophetic spokesperson for the poor. Such a melded identity allowed King to speak not only to white America and to the black poor, but to turn, unhesitatingly, as well to his sisters and brothers in the expanding black middle class. So he spoke with unflinching honesty and undeniable authenticity when he wrote, "It is time for the Negro middle class to rise up from its stool of indifference, to retreat from its flight into unreality and to bring its full resources—its heart, its mind and its checkbook—to the aid of the less fortunate brother [and sister]." (King, here, as in the entire book, unfortunately was a captive of the male gender preferences of his time—and of his church background. When I consider his capacity for growth, I like to believe that if he had been given another decade he would have discovered his own best possibilities there as elsewhere.)

His words to the black middle class provided an excellent opportunity for King to clarify again what he meant by America's constantly used and misused word "integration." He wrote, "Let us not think of our movement as one that seeks to integrate the Negro into all the existing values of American society." Instead, he urged, "Let us be those creative dissenters who will call our beloved nation to a higher destiny, to a new plateau of compassion, to a more noble expression of humanness."

In the light of King's unstintingly accurate critique of his "beloved nation," and his vision of our "higher destiny" as human beings, it was clear why he needed to believe in Tom Paine's radical vision of our capacity "to begin the world over again," moving toward "the final goal" of "genuine intergroup and interpersonal living." Indeed, he seemed deeply in sync with James Baldwin's urgent call to us to "realize ourselves" as an American family of many rich varieties. He was clearly attuned to Langston Hughes's readiness to "swear this oath" that "America will be." Indeed he often seemed the prescient older brother to poet June Jordan and her conviction that "we are the ones we've been waiting for" to transform this reluctant nation into its best possible self.

In fact, reading his words of hope again, I remembered Martin's elder sister-in-struggle, Fannie Lou Hamer, Mississippi's wise and courageous grassroots freedom movement leader who became a gift to us all. I recalled the story of her being questioned by a reporter at the historic 1964 Democratic National Convention and asked about her powerful challenge on behalf of the Mississippi Freedom Democratic Party to the convention's acceptance of segregated delegations. Did her vigorous antisegregation stand mean that "she was seeking equality with the white man?" the reporter asked. "No," Ms. Hamer firmly replied. "What would I look like fighting for equality with the white man? I don't want to go down that low. I want the true democracy that'll raise me *and* the white man up . . . raise America up."

Using somewhat different language, this was the message that King fervently sought to convey to his nation, his people, his children. That was the ultimate answer to the question posed by his book's title *Where Do We Go from Here.* To raise America up, that's where.

So he was urgent about finding a way through the interstices of his horrendous traveling schedule, dealing with dozens of speaking commitments, both in the United States and overseas, calling and attending SCLC strategy sessions, tending to a constant set of internal and external crises in Chicago and Atlanta, always needing to be available for fund-raising gatherings, hurrying toward family rendezvous. Moving through all of that, toward the end of 1966, he pressed himself to finish the manuscript. (Actually, King had been working on it, in many forms, ever since he moved to Chicago in January of that year, often sharing his developing, searching thinking with Clarence Jones, Stanley Levison, Bayard Rustin, and Andrew Young—his most consistent political and literary advisors. Sometimes he shared sections of the emerging manuscript at staff retreats.)

One final step on the way to completion involved what was originally planned as a four-week escape to Jamaica, in January 1967. Carrying several suitcases of notes and other materials, King traveled with his assistant, Bernard Lee, and his impressively competent and committed secretary, Dora McDonald. Coretta also joined him on several occasions during the Jamaica retreat, where he was freed of the telephone and its demands. So he was free to pay even deeper attention, free to continue to wrestle with the amazingly complex systems of devastation and constraint that were faced by poor people in America.

He was also free to speak with loving candor and seething anger to his "white brothers and sisters" who refused to recognize their own deep personal and structural involvement in the causes of the urban rebellions and the call for Black Power. Out of that freedom emerged King's most direct word to white Americans: "Negroes hold only one key to the double lock of peaceful change. The other is in the hands of the white community."

Before the book was finally published in June 1967, King had clearly decided to follow his conscience and his commitment to the poor when, on April 4, in New York's Riverside Church, he raised his voice in an unambiguous, powerful call for America to end its destructive, colonialist-style participation in the Vietnam War. (I am grateful that Martin asked me to prepare the first draft of that statement for him.)

Then, not long after *Where Do We Go from Here* appeared, its beleaguered and determined author began to announce the somewhat vague plans that SCLC was preparing to lead a major campaign of civil disobedience the following spring in Washington, D.C.—a Poor People's Campaign. The plans were to bring thousands of poor Americans to the nation's capital to demand that the War on Poverty receive the energy, funding, and attention that should be withdrawn from the war in Southeast Asia. Significantly, the Poor People of the campaign were meant to include not only African Americans, but whites, Latinos, and Native Americans as well.

For King it was obvious that his answer to the book's subtitle was very clear: a deeply integrated, loving community rather than segregated chaos; hope rather than despair—raising up America and making the world over. While on his committed journey in that humane direction, King was invited to turn his commitment to the poor into a very concrete collaboration with hundreds of exploited, mistreated garbage workers in Memphis, Tennessee. The first paperback version of this book was published shortly after his assassination in the consciously chosen company of the poor.

When the late Coretta King wrote her brief and thoughtful preface to the original, post-assassination Beacon paperback she closed with these words: "The glowing spirit and the sharp insights of Martin Luther King, Jr., are embodied in this book. The solutions he offered can still save our society from self-destruction. I hope that it will be seen as a testament, and that the grief that followed his death will be transmitted to a universal determination to realize the economic and social justice for which he so willingly gave his life."

VINCENT HARDING

FOREWORD

It was characteristic of my husband that in 1967 when confusion in the civil rights struggle abounded he would undertake a book titled *Where Do We Go from Here: Chaos or Community?* He not only took the responsibility for leadership, he toiled vigorously to offer discerning leadership.

In this book he piercingly revealed the cause of our national discord, placing it squarely on the ingrained white racism of American society. He made discrimination and poverty the central focus of his attacks. A year later, spending nearly a million dollars with a huge staff, the National Advisory Commission on Civil Disorders was to come to the same essential conclusions.

In this work Martin Luther King, Jr., stresses the common cause of all the disinherited, white and black, laying the basis for the contemporary struggles now unfolding around economic issues. He spoke out sharply for all the poor in all their hues, for he knew if color made them different, misery and oppression made them the same.

The book is remarkably contemporary also in its treatment of international relations. The author here discusses poverty as a source of world instability and the arrogance of wealthy nations toward the deprived world. It is our common tragedy that we have lost his prophetic voice but it would compound the tragedy if the lessons he did articulate are now ignored.

The glowing spirit and the sharp insights of Martin Luther King, Jr., are embodied in this book. The solutions he offered can still save our society from self-destruction. I hope that it will be seen as a testament, and that the grief that followed his death will be transmuted to a universal determination to realize the economic and social justice for which he so willingly gave his life.

CORETTA SCOTT KING

May 1968

WHERE DO WE GO FROM HERE

I

Where Are We?

On August 6, 1965, the President's Room of the Capitol could scarcely hold the multitude of white and Negro leaders crowding it. President Lyndon Johnson's high spirits were marked as he circulated among the many guests whom he had invited to witness an event he confidently felt to be historic, the signing of the 1965 Voting Rights Act. The legislation was designed to put the ballot effectively into Negro hands in the South after a century of denial by terror and evasion.

The bill that lay on the polished mahogany desk was born in violence in Selma, Alabama, where a stubborn sheriff handling Negroes in the Southern tradition had stumbled against the future. During a nonviolent demonstration for voting rights, the sheriff had directed his men in teargassing and beating the marchers to the ground. The nation had seen and heard, and exploded in indignation. In protest, Negroes and whites marched fifty miles through Alabama, and arrived at the state capital of Montgomery in a demonstration fifty thousand strong. President Johnson, describing Selma as a modern Concord, addressed a joint session of Congress before a television audience of millions. He pledged that "We shall overcome," and declared that the national government must by law insure to every Negro his full rights as a citizen. The Voting Rights Bill of 1965 was the result. In signing the measure, the President announced that "Today is a triumph for freedom as huge as any victory that's ever been won on any battlefield . . . today we strike away the last major shackle of . . . fierce and ancient bonds."

One year later, some of the people who had been brutalized in Selma and who were present at the Capitol ceremonies were leading marchers in the suburbs of Chicago amid a rain of rocks and bottles, among burning automobiles, to the thunder of jeering thousands, many of them waving Nazi flags.

A year later, some of the Negro leaders who had been present in Selma and at the Capitol ceremonies no longer held office in their organizations. They had been discarded to symbolize a radical change of tactics.

A year later, the white backlash had become an emotional electoral issue in California, Maryland and elsewhere. In several Southern states men long regarded as political clowns had become governors or only narrowly missed election, their magic achieved with a "witches'" brew of bigotry, prejudice, half-truths and whole lies.

During the year, white and Negro civil rights workers had been murdered in several Southern communities. The swift and easy acquittals that followed for the accused had shocked much of the nation but sent a wave of unabashed triumph through Southern segregationist circles. Many of us wept at the funeral services for the dead and for democracy.

During the year, in several Northern and Western cities, most tragically in Watts, young Negroes had exploded in violence. In an irrational burst of rage they had sought to say something, but the flames had blackened both themselves and their oppressors.

A year later, *Ramparts* magazine was asserting, "After more than a decade of the Civil Rights Movement the black American in Harlem, Haynesville, Baltimore and Bogalousa is worse off today than he was ten years ago . . . the Movement's leaders know it and it is the source of their despair. . . . The Movement is in despair because it has been forced to recognize the Negro revolution as a myth."

Had Negroes fumbled the opportunities described by the President? Was the movement in despair? Why was widespread sympathy with the Negro revolution abruptly submerged in indifference in some quarters or banished by outright hostility in others? Why was there ideological disarray?

A simple explanation holds that Negroes rioted in Watts, the voice of Black Power was heard through the land and the white backlash was born; the public became infuriated and sympathy evaporated. This pat explanation founders, however, on the hard fact that the change in mood had preceded Watts and the Black Power slogan. Moreover, the white backlash had always existed underneath and sometimes on the surface of American life. No, the answers are both more complex and, for the long run, less pessimistic.

With Selma and the Voting Rights Act one phase of development in the civil rights revolution came to an end. A new phase opened, but few observers realized it or were prepared for its implications. For the vast majority of white Americans, the past decade—the first phase—had been a struggle to treat the Negro with a degree of decency, not of equality. White America was ready to demand that the Negro should be spared the lash of brutality and coarse degradation, but it had never been truly committed to helping him out of poverty, exploitation or all forms of discrimination. The outraged white citizen had been sincere when he snatched the whips from the Southern sheriffs and forbade them more cruelties. But when this was to a degree accomplished, the emotions that had momentarily inflamed him melted away. White Americans left the Negro on the ground and in devastating numbers walked off with the aggressor. It appeared that the white segregationist and the ordinary white citizen had more in common with one another than either had with the Negro.

When Negroes looked for the second phase, the realization of equality, they found that many of their white allies had quietly disappeared. The Negroes of America had taken the President, the press and the pulpit at their word when they spoke in broad terms of freedom and justice. But the absence of brutality and unregenerate evil is not the presence of justice. To stay murder is not the same thing as to ordain brotherhood. The word was broken, and the free-running expectations of the Negro crashed into the stone walls of white resistance. The result was havoc. Negroes felt cheated, especially in the North, while many whites felt that the Negroes had gained so much it was virtually impudent and greedy to ask for more so soon.

The paths of Negro-white unity that had been converging crossed at Selma, and like a giant X began to diverge. Up to Selma there had been unity to eliminate barbaric conduct. Beyond it the unity had to be based on the fulfillment of equality, and in the absence of agreement the paths began inexorably to move apart.

II

Why is equality so assiduously avoided? Why does white America delude itself, and how does it rationalize the evil it retains?

The majority of white Americans consider themselves

sincerely committed to justice for the Negro. They believe that American society is essentially hospitable to fair play and to steady growth toward a middle-class Utopia embodying racial harmony. But unfortunately this is a fantasy of self-deception and comfortable vanity. Overwhelmingly America is still struggling with irresolution and contradictions. It has been sincere and even ardent in welcoming some change. But too quickly apathy and disinterest rise to the surface when the next logical steps are to be taken. Laws are passed in a crisis mood after a Birmingham or a Selma, but no substantial fervor survives the formal signing of legislation. The recording of the law in itself is treated as the reality of the reform.

This limited degree of concern is a reflection of an inner conflict which measures cautiously the impact of any change on the status quo. As the nation passes from opposing extremist behavior to the deeper and more pervasive elements of equality, white America reaffirms its bonds to the status quo. It had contemplated comfortably hugging the shoreline but now fears that the winds of change are blowing it out to sea.

The practical cost of change for the nation up to this point has been cheap. The limited reforms have been obtained at bargain rates. There are no expenses, and no taxes are required, for Negroes to share lunch counters, libraries, parks, hotels and other facilities with whites. Even the psychological adjustment is far from formidable. Having exaggerated the emotional difficulties for decades, when demands for new conduct became inescapable, white Southerners may have trembled under the strain but they did not collapse.

Even the more significant changes involved in voter registration required neither large monetary nor psychological sacrifice. Spectacular and turbulent events that dramatized the demand created an erroneous impression that a heavy burden was involved.

The real cost lies ahead. The stiffening of white resistance is a recognition of that fact. The discount education given Negroes will in the future have to be purchased at full price if quality education is to be realized. Jobs are harder and costlier to create than voting rolls. The eradication of slums housing millions is complex far beyond integrating buses and lunch counters.

The assistant director of the Office of Economic Opportunity, Hyman Bookbinder, in a frank statement on December 29, 1966, declared that the long-range costs of adequately implementing programs to fight poverty, ignorance and slums will reach one trillion dollars. He was not awed or dismayed by this prospect but instead pointed out that the growth of the gross national product during the same period makes this expenditure comfortably possible. It is, he said, as simple as this: "The poor can stop being poor if the rich are willing to become even richer at a slower rate." Furthermore, he predicted that unless a "substantial sacrifice is made by the American people," the nation can expect further deterioration of the cities, increased antagonisms between races and continued disorders in the streets. He asserted that people are not informed enough to give adequate support to antipoverty programs, and he leveled a share of the blame at the government because it "must do more to get people to understand the size of the problem."

Let us take a look at the size of the problem through the lens of the Negro's status in 1967. When the Constitution was written, a strange formula to determine taxes and representation declared that the Negro was 60 percent of a person.[1] Today another curious formula seems to declare he is 50 percent of a person. Of the good things in life he has approximately one-half those of whites; of the bad he has twice those of whites. Thus, half of all Negroes live in substandard housing, and Negroes have half the income of whites. When we turn to the negative experiences of life, the Negro has a double share. There are twice as many unemployed. The rate of infant mortality (widely accepted as an accurate index of general health) among Negroes is double that of whites.[2] The equation pursues Negroes even into war. There were twice as many Negroes as whites in combat in Vietnam at the beginning of 1967, and twice as many Negro soldiers died in action (20.6 percent) in proportion to their numbers in the population.[3]

In other spheres the figures are equally alarming. In elementary schools Negroes lag one to three years behind whites, and their segregated schools receive substantially less money per student than do the white schools. Onetwentieth as many Negroes as whites attend college, and half of these are in ill-equipped Southern institutions.[4]

Of employed Negroes, 75 percent hold menial jobs.[5] Depressed living standards for Negroes are not simply the consequence of neglect. Nor can they be explained by the myth of the Negro's innate incapacities, or by the more sophisticated rationalization of his acquired infirmities (family disorganization, poor education, etc.). They are a structural part of the economic system in the United States. Certain industries and enterprises are based upon a supply of low-paid, under-skilled and immobile nonwhite labor. Hand-assembly factories, hospitals, service industries, housework, agricultural operations using itinerant labor would suffer economic trauma, if not disaster, with a rise in wage scales.

Economic discrimination is especially deeply rooted in the South. In industry after industry there is a significant differential in wage scales between North and South. The lower scale in the South is directly a consequence of cheap Negro labor (which ironically not only deprives the Negro but by its presence drives down the wages of the white worker). The new South, while undergoing certain marked changes as a result of industrialization, is adapting the forms of discrimination that keep the Negro in a subordinate role and hold his wage scales close to the bottom.

The personal torment of discrimination cannot be measured on a numerical scale, but the grim evidence of its hold on white Americans is revealed in polls that indicate that 88 percent of them would object if their teenage child dated a Negro. Almost 80 percent would mind it if a close friend or relative married a Negro, and 50 percent would not want a Negro as a neighbor.[6]

These brief facts disclose the magnitude of the gap between existing realities and the goal of equality. Yet they would be less disturbing if it were not for a greater difficulty. There is not even a common language when the term "equality" is used. Negro and white have a fundamentally different definition.

Negroes have proceeded from a premise that equality means what it says, and they have taken white Americans at their word when they talked of it as an objective. But most whites in America in 1967, including many persons of goodwill, proceed from a premise that equality is a loose expression for improvement. White America is not even psychologically organized to close the gap—essentially it seeks only to make it less painful and less obvious but in most respects to retain it. Most of the abrasions between Negroes and white liberals arise from this fact.

White America is uneasy with injustice and for ten years it believed it was righting wrongs. The struggles were often bravely fought by fine people. The conscience of man flamed high in hours of peril. The days can never be forgotten when the brutalities at Selma caused thousands all over the land to rush to our side, heedless of danger and of differences in race, class and religion.

After the march to Montgomery, there was a delay at the airport and several thousand demonstrators waited more than five hours, crowding together on the seats, the floors and the stairways of the terminal building. As I stood with them and saw white and Negro, nuns and priests, ministers and rabbis, labor organizers, lawyers, doctors, housemaids and shopworkers brimming with vitality and enjoying a rare comradeship, I knew I was seeing a microcosm of the mankind of the future in this moment of luminous and genuine brotherhood.

But these were the best of America, not all of America. Elsewhere the commitment was shallower. Conscience burned only dimly, and when atrocious behavior was curbed, the spirit settled easily into well-padded pockets of complacency. Justice at the deepest level had but few stalwart champions.

A good many observers have remarked that if equality could come at once the Negro would not be ready for it. I submit that the white American is even more unprepared.

The Negro on a mass scale is working vigorously to overcome his deficiencies and his maladjustments. Wherever there are job-training programs Negroes are crowding them. Those who are employed are revealing an eagerness for advancement never before so widespread and persistent. In the average Negro home a new appreciation of culture is manifest. The circulation of periodicals and books written for Negroes is now in the multimillions while a decade ago it was scarcely past one hundred thousand. In the schools more Negro students are demanding courses that lead to college and beyond, refusing to settle for the crude vocational training that limited so many of them in the past.

Whites, it must frankly be said, are not putting in a similar mass effort to reeducate themselves out of their racial ignorance. It is an aspect of their sense of superiority that the white people of America believe they have so little to learn. The reality of substantial investment to assist Negroes into the twentieth century, adjusting to Negro neighbors and genuine school integration, is still a nightmare for all too many white Americans.

White America would have liked to believe that in the past ten years a mechanism had somehow been created that needed only orderly and smooth tending for the painless accomplishment of change. Yet this is precisely what has not been achieved. Every civil rights law is still substantially more dishonored than honored. School desegregation is still 90 percent unimplemented across the land; the free exercise of the franchise is the exception rather than the rule in the South; open-occupancy laws theoretically apply to population centers embracing tens of millions, but grim ghettos contradict the fine language of the legislation. Despite the mandates of law, equal employment still remains a distant dream.

The legal structures have in practice proved to be neither structures nor law. The sparse and insufficient collection of statutes is not a structure; it is barely a naked framework. Legislation that is evaded, substantially nullified and unenforced is a mockery of law. Significant progress has effectively been barred by the cunning obstruction of segregationists. It has been barred by equivocations and retreats of government— the same government that was exultant when it sought political credit for enacting the measures.

In this light, we are now able to see why the Supreme

Court decisions, on school desegregation, which we described at the time as historic, have not made history. After twelve years, barely 12 percent school integration existed in the whole South, and in the Deep South the figure hardly reached 2 percent.[7] And even these few schools were in many cases integrated only with a handful of Negroes. The decisions indeed mandated a profound degree of genuine equality; for that very reason, they failed of implementation. They were, in a sense, historical errors from the point of view of white America.

Even the Supreme Court, despite its original courage and integrity, curbed itself only a little over a year after the 1954 landmark cases, when it handed down its Pupil Placement decision, in effect returning to the states the power to determine the tempo of change. This subsequent decision became the keystone in the structure that slowed school desegregation down to a crawl. Thus America, with segregationist obstruction and majority indifference, silently nibbled away at a promise of true equality that had come before its time.

These are the deepest causes for contemporary abrasions between the races. Loose and easy language about equality, resonant resolutions about brotherhood fall pleasantly on the ear, but for the Negro there is a credibility gap he cannot overlook. He remembers that with each modest advance the white population promptly raises the argument that the Negro has come far enough. Each step forward accents an ever-present tendency to backlash.

This characterization is necessarily general. It would be grossly unfair to omit recognition of a minority of whites who genuinely want authentic equality. Their commitment is real, sincere, and is expressed in a thousand deeds. But they are balanced at the other end of the pole by the unregenerate segregationists who have declared that democracy is not worth having if it involves equality. The segregationist goal is the total reversal of all reforms, with reestablishment of naked oppression and if need be a native form of fascism. America had a master race in the antebellum South. Reestablishing it with a resurgent Klan and a totally disenfranchised lower class would realize the dream of too many extremists on the right.

The great majority of Americans are suspended between these opposing attitudes. They are uneasy with injustice but unwilling yet to pay a significant price to eradicate it.

The persistence of racism in depth and the dawning awareness that Negro demands will necessitate structural changes in society have generated a new phase of white resistance in North and South. Based on the cruel judgment that Negroes have come far enough, there is a strong mood to bring the civil rights movement to a halt or reduce it to a crawl. Negro demands that yesterday evoked admiration and support, today—to many—have become tiresome, unwarranted and a disturbance to the enjoyment of life. Cries of Black Power and riots are not the causes of white resistance, they are consequences of it.

III

Meanwhile frustration and a loss of confidence in white power have engendered among many Negroes a response that is essentially a loss of confidence in themselves. They are failing to appreciate two important facts.

First, the line of progress is never straight. For a period a movement may follow a straight line and then it encounters obstacles and the path bends. It is like curving around a mountain when you are approaching a city. Often it feels as though you were moving backward, and you lose sight of your goal; but in fact you are moving ahead, and soon you will see the city again, closer by.

We are encountering just such an experience today. The inevitable counterrevolution that succeeds every period of progress is taking place. Failing to understand this as a normal process of development, some Negroes are falling into unjustified pessimism and despair. Focusing on the ultimate goal, and discovering it still distant, they declare no progress at all has been made.

This mood illustrates another fact that has been misinterpreted. A final victory is an accumulation of many short-term encounters. To lightly dismiss a success because it does not usher in a complete order of justice is to fail to comprehend the process of achieving full victory. It underestimates the value of confrontation and dissolves the confidence born of a partial victory by which new efforts are powered.

The argument that the Negro has made no progress in a decade of turbulent effort rests on demonstrable facts that paint an ugly picture of stagnation in many areas, including income levels, housing and schools. But from a deeper perspective a different conclusion emerges. The increases in segregated schools and the expanded slums are developments confined largely to the North. Substantial progress has been achieved in the South. The struggles of the past decade were not national in scope; they were Southern; they were specifically designed to change life in the South, and the principal role of the North was supportive. It would be a serious error to misconstrue the movement's strategy by measuring Northern accomplishments when virtually all programs were applied in the South and sought remedies applicable solely to it.

The historic achievement is found in the fact that the

movement in the South has profoundly shaken the entire edifice of segregation. This is an accomplishment whose consequences are deeply felt by every Southern Negro in his daily
life. It is no longer possible to count the number of public
establishments that are open to Negroes. The persistence of
segregation is not the salient fact of Southern experience;
the proliferating areas in which the Negro moves freely is the
new advancing truth.

The South was the stronghold of racism. In the white
migrations through history from the South to the North
and West, racism was carried to poison the rest of the nation. Prejudice, discrimination and bigotry had been intri-
cately imbedded in all institutions of Southern life, political,
social and economic. There could be no possibility of life-
transforming change anywhere so long as the vast and solid
influence of Southern segregation remained unchallenged
and unhurt. The ten-year assault at the roots was fundamental to undermining the system. What distinguished this period from all preceding decades was that it constituted the
first frontal attack on racism at its heart.

Since before the Civil War, the alliance of Southern racism and Northern reaction has been the major roadblock to
all social advancement. The cohesive political structure of
the South working through this alliance enabled a minority of the population to imprint its ideology on the nation's
laws. This explains why the United States is still far behind
European nations in all forms of social legislation. England,
France, Germany, Sweden, all distinctly less wealthy than us,
provide more security relative for their people.

Hence in attacking Southern racism the Negro has already benefited not only himself but the nation as a whole.
Until the disproportionate political power of the reactionary

South in Congress is ended, progress in the United States will always be fitful and uncertain.

Since the beginning of the civil rights revolution, Negro registration in almost every Southern state has increased by at least 100 percent, and in Virginia and Alabama, by 300 and 600 percent, respectively.[8] There are no illusions among Southern segregationists that these gains are unimportant. The old order has already lost ground; its retreats are symbolized by the departure from public life of Sheriffs Clark and Bull Connor. Far more important, the racists have restructured old parties to cope with the emerging challenge. In some states, such as Georgia and Alabama, white supremacy temporarily holds the State House, but it would be a foolish and shortsighted politician who felt secure with this victory. In both of these states the most serious contender in recent elections was a white former governor who publicly welcomed the Negro vote, shaped his policies to it and worked with Negro political organizations in the campaign. This change is itself a revolutionary event. This amazing transformation took place in one decade of struggle after ten decades of virtually total disenfranchisement. The future shape of Southern politics will never again operate without a strong Negro electorate as a significant force.

Even in Mississippi, where electoral advances are not yet marked, a different form of change is manifest. When Negroes decided to march for freedom across the state, they boldly advanced to the capital itself, in a demonstration of thirty thousand people. Ten years before, a Mississippi Negro would have submissively stepped to the gutter to leave the sidewalk for a white man. Ten years before, to plan a meeting, Negroes would have come together at night in the woods as conspirators.

A decade ago, not a single Negro entered the legislative chambers of the South except as a porter or chauffeur. Today eleven Negroes are members of the Georgia House.

Ten years ago, Negroes seemed almost invisible to the larger society, and the facts of their harsh lives were unknown to the majority of the nation. Today civil rights is a dominating issue in every state, crowding the pages of the press and the daily conversation of white Americans.

In this decade of change the Negro stood up and confronted his oppressor—he faced the bullies and the guns, the dogs and the tear gas, he put himself squarely before the vicious mobs and moved with strength and dignity toward them and decisively defeated them.

For more than a century of slavery and another century of segregation Negroes did not find mass unity nor could they mount mass actions. The American brand of servitude tore them apart and held them in paralyzed solitude. But in the last decade Negroes united and marched. And out of the new unity and action vast monuments of dignity were shaped, courage was forged and hope took concrete form.

For hundreds of years Negroes had fought to stay alive by developing an endurance to hardship and heartbreak. In this decade the Negro stepped into a new role. He no longer would endure; he would resist and win. He still had the age-old capacity to live in hunger and want, but now he banished these as his lifelong companions. He could tolerate humiliation and scorn, but now he armed himself with dignity and resistance and his adversary tasted the gall of defeat.

For the first time in his history the Negro did not have to use subterfuge as a defense, or solicit pity. His endurance was not employed for compromise with evil but to supply the strength to crush it.

He came out of his struggle integrated only slightly in the

external society but powerfully integrated within. This was the victory that had to precede all other gains.

He made his government write new laws to alter some of the cruelest injustices that affected him. He made an indifferent and unconcerned nation rise from lethargy and recognize his oppression and struggle with a newly aroused conscience. He gained manhood in the nation that had always called him "boy."

These were the values he won that enlivened hope even while sluggish progress made no substantial changes in the quality or quantity of his daily bread.

The great deal the Negro has won in spiritual undergirding and the great deal he has not won in material progress indicate the strengths and weaknesses in the life of the Negro in 1967. They also reveal that no matter how many obstacles persist the Negro's forward march can no longer be stopped.

The fight is far from over, because it is neither won, as some assert, nor lost, as the calamity-ridden declare.

Negroes have irrevocably undermined the foundations of Southern segregation; they have assembled the power through self-organization and coalition to place their demands on all significant national agendas. And beyond this, they have now accumulated the strength to change the quality and substance of their demands. From issues of personal dignity they are now advancing to programs that impinge upon the basic system of social and economic control. At this level Negro programs go beyond race and deal with economic inequality, wherever it exists. In the pursuit of these goals, the white poor become involved, and the potentiality emerges for a powerful new alliance.

Another momentous gain of the last decade is now being taken for granted. Negroes forged their own tactical theory of nonviolent direct action. It was born in Montgomery, Alabama, and for a time was considered of only limited application. But as it inspired and informed far-flung movements that included sit-ins, boycotts and mass marches, it became clear that a new method of protest action had been born.

When legal contests were the sole form of activity, the ordinary Negro was involved as a passive spectator. His interest was stirred, but his energies were unemployed. Mass marches transformed the common man into the star performer and engaged him in a total commitment. Yet nonviolent resistance caused no explosions of anger—it instigated no riots—it controlled anger and released it under discipline for maximum effect. What lobbying and imploring could not do in legislative halls, marching feet accomplished a thousand miles away. When the Southern Christian Leadership Conference went into Birmingham in 1963, it intended to change that city. But the effect of its campaign was so extensive that President Kennedy was forced to conclude that national legislation was indispensable, and the first civil rights bill with substance was enacted in 1964. Nonviolent direct action had proved to be the most effective generator of change that the movement had seen, and by 1965 all civil rights organizations had embraced it as theirs.

In the past year nonviolent direct action has been pronounced for the tenth time dead. New tactics have been proposed to replace it. The Black Power slogan was described as a doctrine that reached Negro hearts with so deep an appeal that no alternative method could withstand its magnetic force. Rioting was described as a new Negro form of action that evoked results when disciplined demonstration sputtered out against implacable opposition.

Yet Black Power has proved to be a slogan without a program, and with an uncertain following. If it is true that the controversy is not yet resolved, it is also true that no new alternatives to nonviolence within the movement have found viable expression. Confusion has been created, but extensive despair and dissipation of fighting strength have not occurred.

IV

By 1967 the resounding shout of the Negro's protest had shattered the myth of his contentment. The courage with which he confronted enraged mobs dissolved the stereotype of the grinning, submissive Uncle Tom. Indeed, by the end of a turbulent decade there was a new quality to Negro life. The Negro was no longer a subject of change; he was the active organ of change. He powered the drive. He set the pace.

At the same time it had become clear that though white opposition could be defeated it remained a formidable force capable of hardening its resistance when the cost of change was increased.

The daily life of the Negro is still lived in the basement of the Great Society. He is still at the bottom despite the few who have penetrated to slightly higher levels. Even where the door has been forced partially open, mobility for the Negro is still sharply restricted. There is often no bottom at which to start, and when there is, there is almost always no room at the top.

The Northern ghetto dweller still lives in a schizophrenic social milieu. In the past decade he supported and derived pride from Southern struggles and accomplishment. Yet the civil rights revolution appeared to drain energy from the North, energy that flowed South to transform life there while stagnation blanketed Northern Negro communities.

This was a decade of role reversal. The North, heretofore vital, languished, while the traditionally passive South burst with dynamic vigor. The North at best stood still as the South caught up.

Civil rights leaders had long thought the North would benefit derivatively from the Southern struggle. They assumed that without massive upheavals certain systemic changes were inevitable as the whole nation reexamined and searched its conscience. This was a miscalculation. It was founded on the belief that opposition in the North was not intransigent, that it was flexible and was, if not fully, at least partially hospitable to corrective influences. We forgot what we knew daily in the South: freedom is not given, it is won. Concentration of effort in the large Northern cities can no longer be postponed in favor of Southern campaigns. Both must now be sustained.

In assessing the results of the Negro revolution so far, it can be concluded that Negroes have established a foothold, no more. We have written a Declaration of Independence, itself an accomplishment, but the effort to transform the words into a life experience still lies ahead.

The hard truth is that neither Negro nor white has yet done enough to expect the dawn of a new day. While much has been done, it has been accomplished by too few and on a scale too limited for the breadth of the goal. Freedom is not won by a passive acceptance of suffering. Freedom is won by a struggle *against* suffering. By this measure, Negroes have not yet paid the full price for freedom. And whites have not yet faced the full cost of justice.

The brunt of the Negro's past battles was borne by a very small striking force. Though millions of Negroes were ardent and passionate supporters, only a modest number were actively engaged, and these were relatively too few for a broad war against racism, poverty and discrimination. Negroes fought and won, but our engagements were skirmishes, not climactic battles.

No great victories are won in a war for the transformation of a whole people without total participation. Less than this will not create a new society; it will only evoke more sophisticated token amelioration. The Negro has been wrong to toy with the optimistic thought that the breakdown of white resistance could be accomplished at small cost. He will have to do more before his pressure crystallizes new white principles and new responses. The two forces must continue to collide as Negro aspirations burst against the ancient fortresses of the status quo.

This should not be construed as a prediction of violence. On the one hand, there will certainly be new expressions of nonviolent direct action on an enlarged scale. If one hundred thousand Negroes march in a major city to a strategic location, they will make municipal operations difficult to conduct; they will exceed the capacity of even the most reckless local government to use force against them; and they will repeat this action daily if necessary. Without harming persons or property they can draw as much attention to their grievances as the outbreak at Watts, and they will have asserted their unwavering determination while retaining their dignity and discipline.

But on the other hand, it cannot be taken for granted that Negroes will adhere to nonviolence under any and all conditions. When there is rocklike intransigence or sophisticated manipulation that mocks the empty-handed petitioner, rage replaces reason. Nonviolence is a powerful demand for reason and justice. If it is rudely rebuked, it is not transformed into resignation and passivity. Southern segregationists in many places yielded to it because they realized that the alternatives could be intolerable. Northern white leadership has relied too much on tokens and substitutes, and on Negro patience. The end of this road is clearly in sight. The cohesive, potentially explosive Negro community in the North has a short fuse and a long train of abuses. Those who argue that it is hazardous to give warnings, lest the expression of apprehension lead to violence, are in error. Violence has already been practiced too often, and always because remedies were postponed.

It is understandable that the white community should fear the outbreak of riots. They are indefensible as weapons of struggle, and Negroes must sympathize with whites who feel menaced by them. Indeed, Negroes are themselves no less menaced, and those living in the ghetto always suffer most directly from the destructive turbulence of a riot.

Yet the average white person also has a responsibility. He has to resist the impulse to seize upon the rioter as the exclusive villain. He has to rise up with indignation against his own municipal, state and national governments to demand that the necessary reforms be instituted which alone will protect him. If he reserves his resentment only for the Negro, he will be the victim by allowing those who have the greatest culpability to evade responsibility.

Social justice and progress are the absolute guarantors of riot prevention. There is no other answer. Constructive social change will bring certain tranquillity; evasions will merely encourage turmoil.

Negroes hold only one key to the double lock of peaceful change. The other is in the hands of the white community.

II

Black Power

I

"James Meredith has been shot!"

It was about three o'clock in the afternoon on a Monday in June 1966, and I was presiding over the regular staff meeting of the Southern Christian Leadership Conference in our Atlanta headquarters. When we heard that Meredith had been shot in the back only a day after he had begun his Freedom March through Mississippi, there was a momentary hush of anger and dismay throughout the room. Our horror was compounded by the fact that the early reports announced that Meredith was dead. Soon the silence was broken, and from every corner of the room came expressions of outrage. The business of the meeting was forgotten in the shock of this latest evidence that a Negro's life is still worthless in many parts of his own country.

When order was finally restored, our executive staff immediately agreed that the march must continue. After all, we reasoned, Meredith had begun his lonely journey as a pilgrimage against fear. Wouldn't failure to continue only intensify the fears of the oppressed and deprived Negroes of Mississippi? Would this not be a setback for the whole civil rights movement and a blow to nonviolent discipline?

After several calls between Atlanta and Memphis, we

learned that the earlier reports of Meredith's death were false and that he would recover. This news brought relief, but it did not alter our feeling that the civil rights movement had a moral obligation to continue along the path that Meredith had begun.

The next morning I was off to Memphis along with several members of my staff. Floyd McKissick, national director of CORE [Congress of Racial Equality], flew in from New York and joined us on the flight from Atlanta to Memphis. After landing we went directly to the Municipal Hospital to visit Meredith. We were happy to find him resting well. After expressing our sympathy and gratitude for his courageous witness, Floyd and I shared our conviction with him that the march should continue in order to demonstrate to the nation and the world that Negroes would never again be intimidated by the terror of extremist white violence. Realizing that Meredith was often a loner and that he probably wanted to continue the march without a large group, we felt that it would take a great deal of persuasion to convince him that the issue involved the whole civil rights movement. Fortunately, he soon saw this and agreed that we should continue without him. We spent some time discussing the character and logistics of the march, and agreed that we would consult with him daily on every decision.

As we prepared to leave, the nurse came to the door and said, "Mr. Meredith, there is a Mr. Carmichael in the lobby who would like to see you and Dr. King. Should I give him permission to come in?" Meredith consented. Stokely Carmichael entered with his associate, Cleveland Sellers, and immediately reached out for Meredith's hand. He expressed his concern and admiration and brought messages of sympathy from his colleagues in the Student Nonviolent Coordinating Committee. After a brief conversation we all agreed that

James should get some rest and that we should not burden him with any additional talk. We left the room assuring him that we would conduct the march in his spirit and would seek as never before to expose the ugly racism that pervaded Mississippi and to arouse a new sense of dignity and manhood in every Negro who inhabited that bastion of man's inhumanity to man.

In a brief conference Floyd, Stokely and I agreed that the march would be jointly sponsored by CORE, SNCC [Student Nonviolent Coordinating Committee] and SCLC [Southern Christian Leadership Conference], with the understanding that all other civil rights organizations would be invited to join. It was also agreed that we would issue a national call for support and participation.

One hour later, after making staff assignments and setting up headquarters at the Rev. James Lawson's church in Memphis, a group of us packed into four automobiles and made our way to that desolate spot on Highway 51 where James Meredith had been shot the day before. So began the second stage of the Meredith Mississippi Freedom March.

As we walked down the meandering highway in the sweltering heat, there was much talk and many questions were raised.

"I'm not for that nonviolence stuff any more," shouted one of the younger activists.

"If one of these damn white Mississippi crackers touches me, I'm gonna knock the hell out of him," shouted another.

Later on a discussion of the composition of the march came up.

"This should be an all-black march," said one marcher. "We don't need any more white phonies and liberals invading our movement. This is our march."

Once during the afternoon we stopped to sing "We Shall Overcome." The voices rang out with all the traditional fervor, the glad thunder and gentle strength that had always characterized the singing of this noble song. But when we came to the stanza which speaks of "black and white together," the voices of a few of the marchers were muted. I asked them later why they refused to sing that verse. The retort was:

"This is a new day, we don't sing those words any more. In fact, the whole song should be discarded. Not 'We Shall Overcome,' but 'We Shall Overrun.'"

As I listened to all these comments, the words fell on my ears like strange music from a foreign land. My hearing was not attuned to the sound of such bitterness. I guess I should not have been surprised. I should have known that in an atmosphere where false promises are daily realities, where deferred dreams are nightly facts, where acts of unpunished violence toward Negroes are a way of life, nonviolence would eventually be seriously questioned. I should have been reminded that disappointment produces despair and despair produces bitterness, and that the one thing certain about bitterness is its blindness. Bitterness has not the capacity to make the distinction between some and *all*. When some members of the dominant group, particularly those in power, are racist in attitude and practice, bitterness accuses the whole group.

At the end of the march that first day we all went back to Memphis and spent the night in a Negro motel, since we had not yet secured the tents that would serve as shelter each of the following nights on our journey. The discussion continued at the motel. I decided that I would plead patiently with my brothers to remain true to the time-honored principles of our movement. I began with a plea for nonviolence. This immediately aroused some of our friends from the Deacons for Defense, who contended that self-defense was essential and that therefore nonviolence should not be a prerequisite for participation in the march. They were joined in this view by some of the activists from CORE and SNCC.

I tried to make it clear that besides opposing violence on principle, I could imagine nothing more impractical and disastrous than for any of us, through misguided judgment, to precipitate a violent confrontation in Mississippi. We had neither the resources nor the techniques to win. Furthermore, I asserted, many Mississippi whites, from the government on down, would enjoy nothing more than for us to turn to violence in order to use this as an excuse to wipe out scores of Negroes in and out of the march. Finally, I contended that the debate over the question of self-defense was unnecessary since few people suggested that Negroes should not defend themselves as individuals when attacked. The question was not whether one should use his gun when his home was attacked, but whether it was tactically wise to use a gun while participating in an organized demonstration. If they lowered the banner of nonviolence, I said, Mississippi injustice would not be exposed and the moral issues would be obscured.

Next the question of the participation of whites was raised. Stokely Carmichael contended that the inclusion of whites in the march should be de-emphasized and that the dominant appeal should be made for black participation. Others in the room agreed. As I listened to Stokely, I thought about the years that we had worked together in communities all across the South, and how joyously we had then welcomed and accepted our white allies in the movement. What accounted for this reversal in Stokely's philosophy?

I surmised that much of the change had its psychological roots in the experience of SNCC in Mississippi during the summer of 1964, when a large number of Northern white students had come down to help in that racially torn state. What the SNCC workers saw was the most articulate, powerful and self-assured young white people coming to work with the poorest of the Negro people—and simply overwhelming them. That summer Stokely and others in SNCC had probably unconsciously concluded that this was no good for Negroes, for it simply increased their sense of their own inadequacies. Of course, the answer to this dilemma was not to give up, not to conclude that blacks must work with blacks in order for Negroes to gain a sense of their own meaning. The answer was only to be found in persistent trying, perpetual experimentation, persevering togetherness.

Like life, racial understanding is not something that we find but something that we must create. What we find when we enter these mortal plains is existence; but existence is the raw material out of which all life must be created. A productive and happy life is not something that you find; it is something that you make. And so the ability of Negroes and whites to work together, to understand each other, will not be found ready-made; it must be created by the fact of contact.

Along these lines, I implored everyone in the room to see the morality of making the march completely interracial. Consciences must be enlisted in our movement, I said, not merely racial groups. I reminded them of the dedicated whites who had suffered, bled and died in the cause of racial justice, and suggested that to reject white participation now would be a shameful repudiation of all for which they had sacrificed.

Finally, I said that the formidable foe we now faced demanded more unity than ever before and that I would stretch
every point to maintain this unity, but that I could not in
good conscience agree to continue my personal involvement and that of SCLC in the march if it were not publicly
affirmed that it was based on nonviolence and the participation of both black and white. After a few more minutes
of discussion Floyd and Stokely agreed that we could unite
around these principles as far as the march was concerned.
The next morning we had a joint press conference affirming
that the march was nonviolent and that whites were welcomed.

As the days progressed, debates and discussions continued, but they were usually pushed to the background by the
onrush of enthusiasm engendered by the large crowds that
turned out to greet us in every town. We had been marching for about ten days when we passed through Grenada on
the way to Greenwood. Stokely did not conceal his growing
eagerness to reach Greenwood. This was SNCC territory,
in the sense that the organization had worked courageously
there during that turbulent summer of 1964.

As we approached the city, large crowds of old friends
and new turned out to welcome us. At a huge mass meeting
that night, which was held in a city park, Stokely mounted
the platform and after arousing the audience with a powerful
attack on Mississippi justice, he proclaimed: "What we need
is black power." Willie Ricks, the fiery orator of SNCC,
leaped to the platform and shouted, "What do you want?"
The crowd roared, "Black Power." Again and again Ricks
cried, "What do you want?" and the response "Black Power"
grew louder and louder, until it had reached fever pitch.

So Greenwood turned out to be the arena for the birth

of the Black Power slogan in the civil rights movement. The phrase had been used long before by Richard Wright and others, but never until that night had it been used as a slogan in the civil rights movement. For people who had been crushed so long by white power and who had been taught that black was degrading, it had a ready appeal.

Immediately, however, I had reservations about its use. I had the deep feeling that it was an unfortunate choice of words for a slogan. Moreover, I saw it bringing about division within the ranks of the marchers. For a day or two there was fierce competition between those who were wedded to the Black Power slogan and those wedded to Freedom Now. Speakers on each side sought desperately to get the crowds to chant their slogan the loudest.

Sensing this widening split in our ranks, I asked Stokely and Floyd to join me in a frank discussion of the problem. We met the next morning, along with members of each of our staffs, in a small Catholic parish house in Yazoo City. For five long hours I pleaded with the group to abandon the Black Power slogan. It was my contention that a leader has to be concerned about the problem of semantics. Each word, I said, has a denotative meaning—its explicit and recognized sense—and a connotative meaning—its suggestive sense. While the concept of legitimate Black Power might be denotatively sound, the slogan "Black Power" carried the wrong connotations. I mentioned the implications of violence that the press had already attached to the phrase. And I went on to say that some of the rash statements on the part of a few marchers only reinforced this impression.

Stokely replied by saying that the question of violence versus nonviolence was irrelevant. The real question was the need for black people to consolidate their political and economic resources to achieve power. "Power," he said, "is the only thing respected in this world, and we must get it at any cost." Then he looked me squarely in the eye and said, "Martin, you know as well as I do that practically every other ethnic group in America has done just this. The Jews, the Irish and the Italians did it, why can't we?"

"That is just the point," I answered. "No one has ever heard the Jews publicly chant a slogan of Jewish power, but they have power. Through group unity, determination and creative endeavor, they have gained it. The same thing is true of the Irish and Italians. Neither group has used a slogan of Irish or Italian power, but they have worked hard to achieve it. This is exactly what we must do," I said. "We must use every constructive means to amass economic and political power. This is the kind of legitimate power we need. We must work to build racial pride and refute the notion that black is evil and ugly. But this must come through a program, not merely through a slogan."

Stokely and Floyd insisted that the slogan itself was important. "How can you arouse people to unite around a program without a slogan as a rallying cry? Didn't the labor movement have slogans? Haven't we had slogans all along in the freedom movement? What we need is a new slogan with 'black' in it."

I conceded the fact that we must have slogans. But why have one that would confuse our allies, isolate the Negro community and give many prejudiced whites, who might otherwise be ashamed of their anti-Negro feeling, a ready excuse for self-justification?

"Why not use the slogan 'black consciousness' or 'black equality'?" I suggested. "These phrases would be less vulnerable and would more accurately describe what we are about.

The words 'black' and 'power' together give the impression that we are talking about black domination rather than black equality."

Stokely responded that neither would have the ready appeal and persuasive force of Black Power. Throughout the lengthy discussion, Stokely and Floyd remained adamant, and Stokely concluded by saying, with candor, "Martin, I deliberately decided to raise this issue on the march in order to give it a national forum, and force you to take a stand for Black Power."

I laughed. "I have been used before," I said to Stokely. "One more time won't hurt."

The meeting ended with the SCLC staff members still agreeing with me that the slogan was unfortunate and would only divert attention from the evils of Mississippi, while most CORE and SNCC staff members joined Stokely and Floyd in insisting that it should be projected nationally. In a final attempt to maintain unity I suggested that we compromise by not chanting either "Black Power" or "Freedom Now" for the rest of the march. In this way neither the people nor the press would be confused by the apparent conflict, and staff members would not appear to be at loggerheads. They all agreed with this compromise.

But while the chant died out, the press kept the debate going. News stories now centered, not on the injustices of Mississippi, but on the apparent ideological division in the civil rights movement. Every revolutionary movement has its peaks of united activity and its valleys of debate and internal confusion. This debate might well have been little more than a healthy internal difference of opinion, but the press loves the sensational and it could not allow the issue to remain within the private domain of the movement. In

every drama there has to be an antagonist and a protago-
nist, and if the antagonist is not there the press will find and
build one.

II

So Black Power is now a part of the nomenclature of the
national community. To some it is abhorrent, to others dynamic; to some it is repugnant, to others exhilarating; to some
it is destructive, to others it is useful. Since Black Power
means different things to different people and indeed, being
essentially an emotional concept, can mean different things
to the same person on differing occasions, it is impossible to
attribute its ultimate meaning to any single individual or
organization. One must look beyond personal styles, ver-
bal flourishes and the hysteria of the mass media to assess its
values, its assets and liabilities honestly.

First, it is necessary to understand that Black Power is
a cry of disappointment. The Black Power slogan did not
spring full grown from the head of some philosophical Zeus.
It was born from the wounds of despair and disappointment. It is a cry of daily hurt and persistent pain. For centuries the Negro has been caught in the tentacles of white
power. Many Negroes have given up faith in the white majority because "white power" with total control has left them
empty-handed. So in reality the call for Black Power is a
reaction to the failure of white power.

It is no accident that the birth of this slogan in the civil
rights movement took place in Mississippi—the state symbolizing the most blatant abuse of white power. In Mississippi
the murder of civil rights workers is still a popular pastime.
In that state more than forty Negroes and whites have either
been lynched or murdered over the last three years, and not

a single man has been punished for these crimes. More than fifty Negro churches have been burned or bombed in Mississippi in the last two years, yet the bombers still walk the streets surrounded by the halo of adoration.[1] This is white power in its most brutal, cold-blooded and vicious form.

Many of the young people proclaiming Black Power today were but yesterday the devotees of black-white cooperation and nonviolent direct action. With great sacrifice and dedication and a radiant faith in the future they labored courageously in the rural areas of the South; with idealism they accepted blows without retaliating; with dignity they allowed themselves to be plunged into filthy, stinking jail cells; with a majestic scorn for risk and danger they nonviolently confronted the Jim Clarks and the Bull Connors of the South, and exposed the disease of racism in the body politic. If they are America's angry children today, this anger is not congenital. It is a response to the feeling that a real solution is hopelessly distant because of the inconsistencies, resistance and faintheartedness of those in power. If Stokely Carmichael now says that nonviolence is irrelevant, it is because he, as a dedicated veteran of many battles, has seen with his own eyes the most brutal white violence against Negroes and white civil rights workers, and he has seen it go unpunished.

Their frustration is further fed by the fact that even when blacks and whites die together in the cause of justice, the death of the white person gets more attention and concern than the death of the black person. Stokely and his colleagues from SNCC were with us in Alabama when Jimmy Lee Jackson, a brave young Negro man, was killed and when James Reeb, a committed Unitarian white minister, was fatally clubbed to the ground. They remembered how President Johnson sent flowers to the gallant Mrs. Reeb, and in his eloquent "We Shall Overcome" speech paused to mention that one person, James Reeb, had already died in the struggle. Somehow the President forgot to mention Jimmy, who died first. The parents and sister of Jimmy received no flowers from the President. The students felt this keenly. Not that they felt that the death of James Reeb was less than tragic, but because they felt that the failure to mention Jimmy Jackson only reinforced the impression that to white America the life of a Negro is insignificant and meaningless.

There is also great disappointment with the federal government and its timidity in implementing the civil rights laws on its statute books. The gap between promise and fulfillment is distressingly wide. Millions of Negroes are frustrated and angered because extravagant promises made little more than a year ago are a mockery today. When the 1965 Voting Rights Law was signed, it was proclaimed as the dawn of freedom and the open door to opportunity. What was minimally required under the law was the appointment of hundreds of registrars and thousands of federal marshals to inhibit Southern terror. Instead, fewer than sixty registrars were appointed and not a single federal law officer capable of making arrests was sent into the South. As a consequence the old way of life—economic coercion, terrorism, murder and inhuman contempt—has continued unabated. This gulf between the laws and their enforcement is one of the basic reasons why Black Power advocates express contempt for the legislative process.

The disappointment mounts as they turn their eyes to the North. In the Northern ghettos, unemployment, housing discrimination and slum schools mock the Negro who tries to hope. There have been accomplishments and some material gain, but these beginnings have revealed how far we have yet to go. The economic plight of the masses of Negroes has worsened. The gap between the wages of the Negro worker and those of the white worker has widened. Slums are worse and Negroes attend more thoroughly segregated schools today than in 1954.

The Black Power advocates are disenchanted with the inconsistencies in the militaristic posture of our government. Over the last decade they have seen America applauding nonviolence whenever the Negroes have practiced it. They have watched it being praised in the sit-in movements of 1960, in the Freedom Rides of 1961, in the Albany movement of 1962, in the Birmingham movement of 1963 and in the Selma movement of 1965. But then these same black young men and women have watched as America sends black young men to burn Vietnamese with napalm, to slaughter men, women and children; and they wonder what kind of nation it is that applauds nonviolence whenever Negroes face white people in the streets of the United States but then applauds violence and burning and death when these same Negroes are sent to the fields of Vietnam.

All of this represents disappointment lifted to astronomical proportions. It is disappointment with timid white moderates who feel that they can set the timetable for the Negro's freedom. It is disappointment with a federal administration that seems to be more concerned about winning an ill-considered war in Vietnam than about winning the war against poverty here at home. It is disappointment with white legislators who pass laws on behalf of Negro rights that they never intended to implement. It is disappointment with the Christian church that appears to be more white than Christian, and with many white clergymen who prefer to remain silent behind the security of stained-glass windows. It is disappointment with some Negro clergymen who are more concerned about the size of the wheel base on their automobiles than about the quality of their service to the Negro community. It is disappointment with the Negro middle class that has sailed or struggled out of the muddy ponds into the relatively fresh-flowing waters of the mainstream, and in the process has forgotten the stench of the backwaters where their brothers are still drowning.

Second, Black Power, in its broad and positive meaning, is a call to black people to amass the political and economic strength to achieve their legitimate goals. No one can deny that the Negro is in dire need of this kind of legitimate power. Indeed, one of the great problems that the Negro confronts is his lack of power. From the old plantations of the South to the newer ghettos of the North, the Negro has been confined to a life of voicelessness and powerlessness. Stripped of the right to make decisions concerning his life and destiny, he has been subject to the authoritarian and sometimes whimsical decisions of the white power structure. The plantation and the ghetto were created by those who had power both to confine those who had no power and to perpetuate their powerlessness. The problem of transforming the ghetto is, therefore, a problem of power—a confrontation between the forces of power demanding change and the forces of power dedicated to preserving the status quo.

Power, properly understood, is the ability to achieve purpose. It is the strength required to bring about social, political or economic changes. In this sense power is not only desirable but necessary in order to implement the demands of love and justice. One of the greatest problems of history is that the concepts of love and power are usually contrasted as polar opposites. Love is identified with a resignation of power and power with a denial of love. It was this misinterpretation that caused Nietzsche, the philosopher of the "will to power," to reject the Christian concept of love. It was this same misinterpretation which induced Christian theologians to reject Nietzsche's philosophy of the "will to power" in the name of the Christian idea of love. What is needed is a realization that power without love is reckless and abusive and that love without power is sentimental and anemic. Power at its best is love implementing the demands of justice. Justice at its best is love correcting everything that stands against love.

There is nothing essentially wrong with power. The problem is that in America power is unequally distributed. This has led Negro Americans in the past to seek their goals through love and moral suasion devoid of power and white Americans to seek their goals through power devoid of love and conscience. It is leading a few extremists today to advocate for Negroes the same destructive and conscienceless power that they have justly abhorred in whites. It is precisely this collision of immoral power with powerless morality which constitutes the major crisis of our times.

In his struggle for racial justice, the Negro must seek to transform his condition of powerlessness into creative and positive power. One of the most obvious sources of this power is political. In *Why We Can't Wait*[2] I wrote at length of the need for Negroes to unite for political action in order to compel the majority to listen. I urged the development of political awareness and strength in the Negro community, the election of blacks to key positions, and the use of the bloc vote to liberalize the political climate and achieve our just aspirations for freedom and human dignity. To the extent that Black Power advocates these goals, it is a positive and legitimate call to action that we in the civil rights movement have sought to follow all along and which we must intensify in the future.

Black Power is also a call for the pooling of black financial resources to achieve economic security. While the ultimate answer to the Negroes' economic dilemma will be found in a massive federal program for all the poor along the lines of A. Philip Randolph's Freedom Budget, a kind of Marshall Plan for the disadvantaged, there is something that the Negro himself can do to throw off the shackles of poverty. Although the Negro is still at the bottom of the economic ladder, his collective annual income is upwards of $30 billion. This gives him a considerable buying power that can make the difference between profit and loss in many businesses.

Through the pooling of such resources and the development of habits of thrift and techniques of wise investment, the Negro will be doing his share to grapple with his problem of economic deprivation. If Black Power means the development of this kind of strength within the Negro community, then it is a quest for basic, necessary, legitimate power.

Finally, Black Power is a psychological call to manhood. For years the Negro has been taught that he is nobody, that his color is a sign of his biological depravity, that his being has been stamped with an indelible imprint of inferiority, that his whole history has been soiled with the filth of worthlessness. All too few people realize how slavery and racial segregation have scarred the soul and wounded the spirit of the black man. The whole dirty business of slavery was based on the premise that the Negro was a thing to be used, not a person to be respected.

The historian Kenneth Stampp, in his remarkable book *The Peculiar Institution*,[3] has a fascinating section on the psychological indoctrination that was necessary from the master's viewpoint to make a good slave. He gathered the material for this section primarily from the manuals and other documents which were produced by slaveowners on the subject of training slaves. Stampp notes five recurring aspects of this training.

First, those who managed the slaves had to maintain strict discipline. One master said, "Unconditional submission is the only footing upon which slavery should be placed." Another said, "The slave must know that his master is to govern absolutely and he is to obey implicitly, that he is never, for a moment, to exercise either his will or judgment in opposition to a positive order." Second, the masters felt that they had to implant in the bondsman a consciousness of personal inferiority. This sense of inferiority was deliberately extended to his past. The slaveowners were convinced that in order to control the Negroes, the slaves "had to feel that African ancestry tainted them, that their color was a badge of degradation." The third step in the training process was to awe the slaves with a sense of the masters' enormous power. It was necessary, various owners said, "to make them stand in fear." The fourth aspect was the attempt to "persuade the bondsman to take an interest in the master's enterprise and to accept his standards of good conduct." Thus the master's criteria of what was good and true and beautiful were to be accepted unquestioningly by the slaves. The final step, according to Stampp's documents, was "to impress Negroes with their helplessness: to create in them a habit of perfect dependence upon their masters."

Here, then, was the way to produce a perfect slave. Accustom him to rigid discipline, demand from him unconditional submission, impress upon him a sense of his innate inferiority, develop in him a paralyzing fear of white men, train him to adopt the master's code of good behavior, and instill in him a sense of complete dependence.

Out of the soil of slavery came the psychological roots of

the Black Power cry. Anyone familiar with the Black Power movement recognizes that defiance of white authority and white power is a constant theme; the defiance almost becomes a kind of taunt. Underneath it, however, there is a legitimate concern that the Negro break away from "unconditional submission" and thereby assert his own selfhood.

Another obvious reaction of Black Power to the American system of slavery is the determination to glory in blackness and to resurrect joyously the African past. In response to the emphasis on their masters' "enormous power," Black Power advocates contend that the Negro must develop his own sense of strength. No longer are "fear, awe and obedience" to rule. This accounts for, though it does not justify, some Black Power advocates who encourage contempt and even uncivil disobedience as alternatives to the old patterns of slavery. Black Power assumes that Negroes will be slaves unless there is a new power to counter the force of the men who are still determined to be masters rather than brothers.

It is in the context of the slave tradition that some of the ideologues of the Black Power movement call for the need to develop new and indigenous codes of justice for the ghettos, so that blacks may move entirely away from their former masters' "standards of good conduct." Those in the Black Power movement who contend that blacks should cut themselves off from every level of dependence upon whites for advice, money or other help are obviously reacting against the slave pattern of "perfect dependence" upon the masters.

Black Power is a psychological reaction to the psychological indoctrination that led to the creation of the perfect slave. While this reaction has often led to negative and unrealistic responses and has frequently brought about intemperate words and actions, one must not overlook the positive value in calling the Negro to a new sense of manhood, to a deep feeling of racial pride and to an audacious appreciation of his heritage. The Negro must be grasped by a new realization of his dignity and worth. He must stand up amid a system that still oppresses him and develop an unassailable and majestic sense of his own value. He must no longer be ashamed of being black.

The job of arousing manhood within a people that have been taught for so many centuries that they are nobody is not easy. Even semantics have conspired to make that which is black seem ugly and degrading. In *Roget's Thesaurus* there are some 120 synonyms for "blackness" and at least 60 of them are offensive—such words as "blot," "soot," "grime," "devil" and "foul." There are some 134 synonyms for "whiteness," and all are favorable, expressed in such words as "purity," "cleanliness," "chastity" and "innocence." A white lie is better than a black lie. The most degenerate member of a family is the "black sheep," not the "white sheep." Ossie Davis has suggested that maybe the English language should be "reconstructed" so that teachers will not be forced to teach the Negro child 60 ways to despise himself and thereby perpetuate his false sense of inferiority and the white child 134 ways to adore himself and thereby perpetuate his false sense of superiority.

The history books, which have almost completely ignored the contribution of the Negro in American history, have only served to intensify the Negroes' sense of worthlessness and to augment the anachronistic doctrine of white supremacy. All too many Negroes and whites are unaware of the fact that the first American to shed blood in the revolution which freed this country from British oppression was a black seaman named Crispus Attucks. Negroes and whites are almost totally oblivious of the fact that it was a Negro physician, Dr. Daniel Hale Williams, who performed the first successful operation on the heart in America, and that another Negro physician, Dr. Charles Drew, was largely responsible for developing the method of separating blood plasma and storing it on a large scale, a process that saved thousands of lives in World War II and has made possible many of the important advances in postwar medicine. History books have virtually overlooked the many Negro scientists and inventors who have enriched American life. Although a few refer to George Washington Carver, whose research in agricultural products helped to revive the economy of the South when the throne of King Cotton began to totter, they ignore the contribution of Norbert Rillieux, whose invention of an evaporating pan revolutionized the process of sugar refining. How many people know that the multimillion-dollar United Shoe Machinery Company developed from the shoe-lasting machine invented in the last century by a Negro from Dutch Guiana, Jan Matzeliger; or that Granville T. Woods, an expert in electric motors, whose many patents speeded the growth and improvement of the railroads at the beginning of this century, was a Negro?

Even the Negroes' contribution to the music of America is sometimes overlooked in astonishing ways. Two years ago my oldest son and daughter entered an integrated school in Atlanta. A few months later my wife and I were invited to attend a program entitled "Music That Has Made America Great." As the evening unfolded, we listened to the folk songs and melodies of the various immigrant groups. We were certain that the program would end with the most original of all American music, the Negro spiritual. But we were mistaken. Instead, all the students, including our children, ended the program by singing "Dixie."

As we rose to leave the hall, my wife and I looked at each other with a combination of indignation and amazement.

All the students, black and white, all the parents present that night, and all the faculty members had been victimized by just another expression of America's penchant for ignoring the Negro, making him invisible and making his contributions insignificant. I wept within that night. I wept for my children and all black children who have been denied a knowledge of their heritage; I wept for all white children, who, through daily miseducation, are taught that the Negro is an irrelevant entity in American society; I wept for all the white parents and teachers who are forced to overlook the fact that the wealth of cultural and technological progress in America is a result of the commonwealth of inpouring contributions.

The tendency to ignore the Negro's contribution to American life and strip him of his personhood is as old as the earliest history books and as contemporary as the morning's newspaper. To offset this cultural homicide, the Negro must rise up with an affirmation of his own Olympian manhood. Any movement for the Negro's freedom that overlooks this necessity is only waiting to be buried. As long as the mind is enslaved the body can never be free. Psychological freedom, a firm sense of self-esteem, is the most powerful weapon against the long night of physical slavery. No Lincolnian Emancipation Proclamation or Kennedyan or Johnsonian civil rights bill can totally bring this kind of freedom. The Negro will only be truly free when he reaches down to the inner depths of his own being and signs with the pen and ink of assertive selfhood his own emancipation proclamation. With a spirit straining toward true self-esteem, the Negro must boldly throw off the manacles of self-abnegation and say to himself and the world: "I am somebody. I am a person. I am a man with dignity and honor. I have a rich and noble history, however painful and exploited that history has been. I am black *and* comely." This self-affirmation is the black man's need made compelling by the white man's crimes against him. This is positive and necessary power for black people.

III

Nevertheless, in spite of the positive aspects of Black Power, which are compatible with what we have sought to do in the civil rights movement all along without the slogan, its negative values, I believe, prevent it from having the substance and program to become the basic strategy for the civil rights movement in the days ahead.

Beneath all the satisfaction of a gratifying slogan, Black Power is a nihilistic philosophy born out of the conviction that the Negro can't win. It is, at bottom, the view that American society is so hopelessly corrupt and enmeshed in evil that there is no possibility of salvation from within. Although this thinking is understandable as a response to a white power structure that never completely committed itself to true equality for the Negro, and a die-hard mentality that sought to shut all windows and doors against the winds of change, it nonetheless carries the seeds of its own doom.

Before this century, virtually all revolutions had been based on hope and hate. The hope was expressed in the rising expectation of freedom and justice. The hate was an expression of bitterness toward the perpetrators of the old order. It was the hate that made revolutions bloody and violent. What was new about Mahatma Gandhi's movement in India was that he mounted a revolution on hope and love, hope and nonviolence. This same new emphasis characterized the civil rights movement in our country dating from the Montgomery bus boycott of 1956 to the Selma movement of 1965. We maintained the hope while transforming the hate of traditional revolutions into positive nonviolent power. As long as the hope was fulfilled there was little questioning of nonviolence. But when the hopes were blasted, when people came to see that in spite of progress their conditions were still insufferable, when they looked out and saw more poverty, more school segregation and more slums, despair began to set in.

Unfortunately, when hope diminishes, the hate is often turned most bitterly toward those who originally built up the hope. In all the speaking that I have done in the United States before varied audiences, including some hostile whites, the only time that I have been booed was one night in a Chicago mass meeting by some young members of the Black Power movement. I went home that night with an ugly feeling. Selfishly I thought of my sufferings and sacrifices over the last twelve years. Why would they boo one so close to them? But as I lay awake thinking, I finally came to myself, and I could not for the life of me have less than patience and understanding for those young people. For twelve years I, and others like me, had held out radiant promises of progress. I had preached to them about my dream. I had lectured to them about the not too distant day when they would have freedom, "all, here and now." I had urged them to have faith in America and in white society. Their hopes had soared. They were now booing because they felt that we were unable to deliver on our promises. They were booing because we had urged them to have faith in people who had too often proved to be unfaithful. They were now hostile because they were watching the dream that they had so readily accepted turn into a frustrating nightmare.

But revolution, though born of despair, cannot long be sustained by despair. This is the ultimate contradiction of the Black Power movement. It claims to be the most revolutionary wing of the social revolution taking place in the United States. Yet it rejects the one thing that keeps the fire of revolutions burning: the ever-present flame of hope. When hope dies, a revolution degenerates into an undiscriminating catchall for evanescent and futile gestures. The Negro cannot entrust his destiny to a philosophy nourished solely on despair, to a slogan that cannot be implemented into a program.

The Negro's disappointment is real and a part of the daily menu of our lives. One of the most agonizing problems of human experience is how to deal with disappointment. In our individual lives we all too often distill our frustrations into an essence of bitterness, or drown ourselves in the deep waters of self-pity, or adopt a fatalistic philosophy that whatever happens must happen and all events are determined by necessity. These reactions poison the soul and scar the personality, always harming the person who harbors them more than anyone else. The only healthy answer lies in one's honest recognition of disappointment even as he still clings to hope, one's acceptance of finite disappointment even while clinging to infinite hope.

We Negroes, who have dreamed for so long of freedom, are still confined in a prison of segregation and discrimination. Must we respond with bitterness and cynicism? Certainly not, for this can lead to black anger so desperate that it ends in black suicide. Must we turn inward in self-pity? Of course not, for this can lead to a self-defeating black paranoia. Must we conclude that we cannot win? Certainly not, for this will lead to a black nihilism that seeks disruption for disruption's sake. Must we, by fatalistically concluding that segregation is a foreordained pattern of the universe, resign ourselves to oppression? Of course not, for passively to co-operate with an unjust system makes the oppressed as evil as the oppressors. Our most fruitful course is to stand firm, move forward nonviolently, accept disappointments and cling to hope. Our determined refusal not to be stopped will eventually open the door to fulfillment. By recognizing the necessity of suffering in a righteous cause, we may achieve our humanity's full stature. To guard ourselves from bitterness, we need the vision to see in this generation's ordeals the opportunity to transfigure both ourselves and American society.

In 1956 I flew from New York to London in the propeller-type aircraft that required nine and a half hours for a flight now made in six hours by jet. Returning from London to the United States, the stewardess announced that the flying time would be twelve and a half hours. The distance was the same. Why an additional three hours? When the pilot entered the cabin to greet the passengers, I asked him to explain.

"You must understand about the winds," he said. "When we leave New York, a strong tail wind is in our favor, but when we return, a strong head wind is against us." Then he added, "Don't worry. These four engines are capable of battling the winds."

In any social revolution there are times when the tail winds of triumph and fulfillment favor us, and other times when strong head winds of disappointment and setbacks beat against us relentlessly. We must not permit adverse winds to overwhelm us as we journey across life's mighty Atlantic; we must be sustained by our engines of courage in spite of the winds. This refusal to be stopped, this "courage to be," this determination to go on "in spite of" is the hallmark of any great movement.

The Black Power movement of today, like the Garvey "Back to Africa" movement of the 1920s, represents a dashing of hope, a conviction of the inability of the Negro to win and a belief in the infinitude of the ghetto. While there is much grounding in past experience for all these feelings, a revolution cannot succumb to any of them. Today's despair is a poor chisel to carve out tomorrow's justice.

Black Power is an implicit and often explicit belief in black separatism. Notice that I do not call it black racism. It is inaccurate to refer to Black Power as racism in reverse, as some have recently done. Racism is a doctrine of the congenital inferiority and worthlessness of a people. While a few angry proponents of Black Power have, in moments of bitterness, made wild statements that come close to this kind of racism, the major proponents of Black Power have never contended that the white man is innately worthless.

Yet behind Black Power's legitimate and necessary concern for group unity and black identity lies the belief that there can be a separate black road to power and fulfillment. Few ideas are more unrealistic. There is no salvation for the Negro through isolation.

One of the chief affirmations of Black Power is the call for the mobilization of political strength for black people. But we do not have to look far to see that effective political power for Negroes cannot come through separatism. Granted that there are cities and counties in the country where the Negro is in a majority, they are so few that concentration on them alone would still leave the vast majority of Negroes outside the mainstream of American political life.

Out of the eighty-odd counties in Alabama, the state where SNCC sought to develop an all-black party, only nine have a majority of Negroes. Even if blacks could control each of these counties, they would have little influence in over-all state politics and could do little to improve conditions in the major Negro population centers of Birmingham, Mobile and Montgomery. There are still relatively few congressional districts in the South that have such large black majorities that Negro candidates could be elected without the aid of whites. Is it a sounder program to concentrate on the election of two or three Negro congressmen from predominantly Negro districts or to concentrate on the election of fifteen or twenty Negro congressmen from Southern districts where a coalition of Negro and white moderate voters is possible?

Moreover, any program that elects all black candidates simply because they are black and rejects all white candidates simply because they are white is politically unsound and morally unjustifiable. It is true that in many areas of the South Negroes still must elect Negroes in order to be effectively represented. SNCC staff members are eminently correct when they point out that in Lowndes County, Alabama, there are no white liberals or moderates and no possibility for cooperation between the races at the present time. But the Lowndes County experience cannot be made a measuring rod for the whole of America. The basic thing in determining the best candidate is not his color but his integrity.

Black Power alone is no more insurance against social injustice than white power. Negro politicians can be as opportunistic as their white counterparts if there is not an informed and determined constituency demanding social reform. What is most needed is a coalition of Negroes and liberal whites that will work to make both major parties truly responsive to the needs of the poor. Black Power does not envision or desire such a program.

Just as the Negro cannot achieve political power in isolation, neither can he gain economic power through separatism. While there must be a continued emphasis on the need for blacks to pool their economic resources and withdraw consumer support from discriminating firms, we must not be oblivious to the fact that the larger economic problems confronting the Negro community will only be solved by federal programs involving billions of dollars. One unfortunate thing about Black Power is that it gives priority to race precisely at a time when the impact of automation and other forces have made the economic question fundamental for blacks and whites alike. In this context a slogan "Power for Poor People" would be much more appropriate than the slogan "Black Power."

However much we pool our resources and "buy black," this cannot create the multiplicity of new jobs and provide the number of low-cost houses that will lift the Negro out of the economic depression caused by centuries of deprivation. Neither can our resources supply quality integrated education. All of this requires billions of dollars which only an alliance of liberal-labor-civil-rights forces can stimulate. In short, the Negroes' problem cannot be solved unless the whole of American society takes a new turn toward greater economic justice.

In a multiracial society no group can make it alone. It is a myth to believe that the Irish, the Italians and the Jews—the ethnic groups that Black Power advocates cite as justification for their views—rose to power through separatism. It is true that they stuck together. But their group unity was always enlarged by joining in alliances with other groups such as political machines and trade unions. To succeed in a pluralistic society, and an often hostile one at that, the Negro obviously needs organized strength, but that strength will only be effective when it is consolidated through constructive alliances with the majority group.

Those proponents of Black Power who have urged Negroes to shun alliances with whites argue that whites as a group cannot have a genuine concern for Negro progress. Therefore, they claim, the white man's main interest in collaborative effort is to diminish Negro militancy and deflect it from constructive goals.

Undeniably there are white elements that cannot be trusted, and no militant movement can afford to relax its vigilance against halfhearted associates or conscious betrayers. Every alliance must be considered on its own merits. Negroes may embrace some and walk out on others where their interests are imperiled. Occasional betrayals, however, do not justify the rejection of the principle of Negro-white alliance.

The oppression of Negroes by whites has left an understandable residue of suspicion. Some of this suspicion is a healthy and appropriate safeguard. An excess of skepticism, however, becomes a fetter. It denies that there can be reliable white allies, even though some whites have died heroically at the side of Negroes in our struggle and others have risked economic and political peril to support our cause.

The history of the movement reveals that Negro-white alliances have played a powerfully constructive role, especially in recent years. While Negro initiative, courage and imagination precipitated the Birmingham and Selma confrontations and revealed the harrowing injustice of segregated life, the organized strength of Negroes alone would have been insufficient to move Congress and the administration without the weight of the aroused conscience of white America. In the period ahead Negroes will continue to need this support. Ten percent of the population cannot by tensions alone induce 90 percent to change a way of life.

Within the white majority there exists a substantial group who cherish democratic principles above privilege and who have demonstrated a will to fight side by side with the Negro against injustice. Another and more substantial group is composed of those having common needs with the Negro and who will benefit equally with him in the achievement of social progress. There are, in fact, more poor white Americans than there are Negro. Their need for a war on poverty is no less desperate than the Negro's. In the South they have been deluded by race prejudice and largely remained aloof from common action. Ironically, with this posture they were fighting not only the Negro but themselves. Yet there are already signs of change. Without formal alliances, Negroes and whites have supported the same candidates in many de facto electoral coalitions in the South because each sufficiently served his own needs.

The ability of Negroes to enter alliances is a mark of our growing strength, not of our weakness. In entering an alliance, the Negro is not relying on white leadership or ideology; he is taking his place as an equal partner in a common endeavor. His organized strength and his new independence pave the way for alliances. Far from losing independence in an alliance, he is using it for constructive and multiplied gains.

Negroes must shun the very narrow-mindedness that in others has so long been the source of our own afflictions. We have reached the stage of organized strength and independence to work securely in alliances. History has demonstrated with major victories the effectiveness, wisdom and moral soundness of Negro-white alliance. The cooperation of Negro and white based on the solid ground of honest conscience and proper self-interest can continue to grow in scope and influence. It can attain the strength to alter basic institutions by democratic means. Negro isolation can never approach this goal.

In the final analysis the weakness of Black Power is its failure to see that the black man needs the white man and the white man needs the black man. However much we may try to romanticize the slogan, there is no separate black path to power and fulfillment that does not intersect white paths, and there is no separate white path to power and fulfillment, short of social disaster, that does not share that power with black aspirations for freedom and human dignity. We are bound together in a single garment of destiny. The language, the cultural patterns, the music, the material prosperity and even the food of America are an amalgam of black and white.

James Baldwin once related how he returned home from school and his mother asked him whether his teacher was colored or white. After a pause he answered: "She is a little bit colored and a little bit white."[4] This is the dilemma of being a Negro in America. In physical as well as cultural terms every Negro is a little bit colored and a little bit white. In our search for identity we must recognize this dilemma.

Every man must ultimately confront the question "Who am I?" and seek to answer it honestly. One of the first principles of personal adjustment is the principle of self-acceptance. The Negro's greatest dilemma is that in order to be healthy he must accept his ambivalence. The Negro is the child of two cultures—Africa and America. The problem is that in the search for wholeness all too many Negroes seek to embrace only one side of their natures. Some, seeking to reject their heritage, are ashamed of their color, ashamed of black art and music, and determine what is beautiful and good by the standards of white society. They end up frustrated and without cultural roots. Others seek to reject everything American and to identify totally with Africa, even to the point of wearing African clothes. But this approach leads also to frustration because the American Negro is not an African. The old Hegelian synthesis still offers the best answer to many of life's dilemmas. The American Negro is neither totally African nor totally Western. He is Afro-American, a true hybrid, a combination of two cultures.

Who are we? We are the descendants of slaves. We are the offspring of noble men and women who were kidnaped from their native land and chained in ships like beasts. We are the heirs of a great and exploited continent known as Africa. We are the heirs of a past of rope, fire and murder. I for one am not ashamed of this past. My shame is for those who became so inhuman that they could inflict this torture upon us.

But we are also Americans. Abused and scorned though we may be, our destiny is tied up with the destiny of America. In spite of the psychological appeals of identification with Africa, the Negro must face the fact that America is now his home, a home that he helped to build through "blood, sweat and tears." Since we are Americans the solution to our problem will not come through seeking to build a separate black nation within a nation, but by finding that creative minority of the concerned from the ofttimes apathetic majority, and together moving toward that colorless power that we all need for security and justice.

In the first century BC, Cicero said: "Freedom is participation in power." Negroes should never want all power because they would deprive others of their freedom. By the same token, Negroes can never be content without participation in power. America must be a nation in which its multiracial people are partners in power. This is the essence of democracy toward which all Negro struggles have been directed since the distant past when he was transplanted here in chains.

Probably the most destructive feature of Black Power is its unconscious and often conscious call for retaliatory violence. Many well-meaning persons within the movement rationalize that Black Power does not really mean black violence, that those who shout the slogan don't really mean it that way, that the violent connotations are solely the distortions of a vicious press. That the press has fueled the fire is true. But as one who has worked and talked intimately with devotees of Black Power, I must admit that the slogan is mainly used by persons who have lost faith in the method and philosophy of nonviolence. I must make it clear that no guilt by association is intended. Both Floyd McKissick and Stokely Carmichael have declared themselves opponents of aggressive violence. This clarification is welcome and useful, despite the persistence of some of their followers in examining the uses of violence.

Over cups of coffee in my home in Atlanta and my apartment in Chicago, I have often talked late at night and over into the small hours of the morning with proponents of Black Power who argued passionately about the validity of violence and riots. They don't quote Gandhi or Tolstoy. Their Bible is Frantz Fanon's *The Wretched of the Earth*.[5] This black psychiatrist from Martinique, who went to Algeria to work with the National Liberation Front in its fight against the French, argues in his book—a well-written book, incidentally, with many penetrating insights—that violence is a psychologically healthy and tactically sound method for the oppressed. And so, realizing that they are a part of that vast company of the "wretched of the earth," these young American Negroes, who are predominantly involved in the Black Power movement, often quote Fanon's belief that violence is the only thing that will bring about liberation. As they say, "Sing us no songs of nonviolence, sing us no songs of progress, for nonviolence and progress belong to middle-class Negroes and whites and we are not interested in you."

As we have seen, the first public expression of disenchantment with nonviolence arose around the question of "self-defense." In a sense this is a false issue, for the right to defend one's home and one's person when attacked has been guaranteed through the ages by common law. In a nonviolent demonstration, however, self-defense must be approached from another perspective.

The cause of a demonstration is the existence of some form of exploitation or oppression that has made it necessary for men of courage and goodwill to protest the evil. For example, a demonstration against de facto school segregation is based on the awareness that a child's mind is crippled by inadequate educational opportunities. The demonstrator agrees that it is better to suffer publicly for a short time to end the crippling evil of school segregation than to have generation after generation of children suffer in ignorance. In such a demonstration the point is made that the schools are inadequate. This is the evil one seeks to dramatize; anything else distracts from that point and interferes with the confrontation of the primary evil. Of course no one wants to suffer and be hurt. But it is more important to get at the cause than to be safe. It is better to shed a little blood from a blow on the head or a rock thrown by an angry mob than to have children by the thousands finishing high school who can only read at a sixth-grade level.

Furthermore, it is dangerous to organize a movement around self-defense. The line of demarcation between defensive violence and aggressive violence is very thin. The minute a program of violence is enunciated, even for self-defense, the atmosphere is filled with talk of violence, and the words falling on unsophisticated ears may be interpreted as an invitation to aggression.

One of the main questions that the Negro must confront in his pursuit of freedom is that of effectiveness. What is the most effective way to achieve the desired goal? If a method is not effective, no matter how much steam it releases, it is an expression of weakness, not of strength. Now the plain, inexorable fact is that any attempt of the American Negro to overthrow his oppressor with violence will not work. We do not need President Johnson to tell us this by reminding Negro rioters that they are outnumbered ten to one. The courageous efforts of our own insurrectionist brothers, such as Denmark Vesey and Nat Turner, should be eternal reminders to us that violent rebellion is doomed from the start. In violent warfare one must be prepared to face the fact that there will be casualties by the thousands. Anyone leading a violent rebellion must be willing to make an honest assessment regarding the possible casualties to a minority population confronting a well-armed, wealthy majority with a fanatical right wing that would delight in exterminating thousands of black men, women and children.

Arguments that the American Negro is a part of a world which is two-thirds colored and that there will come a day when the oppressed people of color will violently rise together to throw off the yoke of white oppression are beyond the realm of serious discussion. There is no colored nation, including China, that now shows even the potential of leading a violent revolution of color in any international proportions. Ghana, Zambia, Tanganyika and Nigeria are so busy fighting their own battles against poverty, illiteracy and the subversive influence of neocolonialism that they offer little hope to Angola, Southern Rhodesia and South Africa, much less to the American Negro. The hard cold facts today indicate that the hope of the people of color in the world may well rest on the American Negro and his ability to reform the structure of racist imperialism from within and thereby turn the technology and wealth of the West to the task of liberating the world from want.

The futility of violence in the struggle for racial justice has been tragically etched in all the recent Negro riots. There is something painfully sad about a riot. One sees screaming youngsters and angry adults fighting hopelessly and aimlessly against impossible odds. Deep down within them you perceive a desire for self-destruction, a suicidal longing. Occasionally Negroes contend that the 1965 Watts riot and the other riots in various cities represented effective civil rights action. But those who express this view always end up with stumbling words when asked what concrete gains have been won as a result. At best the riots have produced a little additional antipoverty money, allotted by frightened government officials, and a few water sprinklers to cool the children of the ghettos. It is something like improving the food in a prison while the people remain securely incarcerated behind bars. Nowhere have the riots won any concrete improvement such as have the organized protest demonstrations.

It is not overlooking the limitations of nonviolence and the distance we have yet to go to point out the remarkable record of achievements that have already come through nonviolent action. The 1960 sit-ins desegregated lunch counters in more than 150 cities within a year. The 1961 Freedom Rides put an end to segregation in interstate travel. The 1956 bus boycott in Montgomery, Alabama, ended segregation on the buses not only of that city but in practically every city of the South. The 1963 Birmingham movement and the climactic March on Washington won passage of the most powerful civil rights law in a century. The 1965 Selma movement brought enactment of the Voting Rights Law. Our nonviolent marches in Chicago last summer brought about a housing agreement which, if implemented, will be the strongest step toward open housing taken in any city in the nation. Most significant is the fact that this progress occurred with minimum human sacrifice and loss of life. Fewer people have been killed in ten years of nonviolent demonstrations across the South than were killed in one night of rioting in Watts.

When one tries to pin down advocates of violence as to what acts would be effective, the answers are blatantly illogical. Sometimes they talk of overthrowing racist state and local governments. They fail to see that no internal revolution has ever succeeded in overthrowing a government by violence unless the government had already lost the allegiance and effective control of its armed forces. Anyone in his right mind knows that this will not happen in the United States. In a violent racial situation, the power structure has the local police, the state troopers, the national guard and finally the army to call on, all of which are predominantly white.

Furthermore, few if any violent revolutions have been successful unless the violent minority had the sympathy and support of the nonresisting majority. Castro may have had only a few Cubans actually fighting with him, but he would never have overthrown the Batista regime unless he had had the sympathy of the vast majority of the Cuban people. It is perfectly clear that a violent revolution on the part of American blacks would find no sympathy and support from the white population and very little from the majority of the Negroes themselves.

This is no time for romantic illusions and empty philosophical debates about freedom. This is a time for action.

What is needed is a strategy for change, a tactical program that will bring the Negro into the mainstream of American life as quickly as possible. So far, this has only been offered by the nonviolent movement. Without recognizing this we will end up with solutions that don't solve, answers that don't answer and explanations that don't explain.

Beyond the pragmatic invalidity of violence is its inability to appeal to conscience. Some Black Power advocates consider an appeal to conscience irrelevant. A Black Power exponent said to me not long ago: "To hell with conscience and morality. We want power." But power and morality must go together, implementing, fulfilling and ennobling each other. In the quest for power I cannot bypass the concern for morality. I refuse to be driven to a Machiavellian cynicism with respect to power. Power at its best is the right use of strength. The words of Alfred the Great are still true: "Power is never good unless he who has it is good."

Nonviolence is power, but it is the right and good use of power. Constructively it can save the white man as well as the Negro. Racial segregation is buttressed by such irrational fears as loss of preferred economic privilege, altered social status, intermarriage and adjustment to new situations. Through sleepless nights and haggard days numerous white people struggle pitifully to combat these fears. By following the path of escape, some seek to ignore the questions of race relations and to close their minds to the issues involved. Others, placing their faith in legal maneuvers, counsel massive resistance. Still others hope to drown their fears by engaging in acts of meanness and violence toward their Negro brethren. But how futile are all these remedies! Instead of eliminating fear, they instill deeper and more pathological fears. The white man, through his own efforts, through education and goodwill, through searching his conscience and through confronting the fact of integration, must do a great deal to free himself of these paralyzing fears. But to master fear he must also depend on the spirit the Negro generates toward him. Only through our adherence to nonviolence— which also means love in its strong and commanding sense —will the fear in the white community be mitigated.

A guilt-ridden white minority fears that if the Negro attains power, he will without restraint or pity act to revenge the accumulated injustices and brutality of the years. The Negro must show that the white man has nothing to fear, for the Negro is willing to forgive. A mass movement exercising nonviolence and demonstrating power under discipline should convince the white community that as such a movement attained strength, its power would be used creatively and not for revenge.

In a moving letter to his nephew on the one hundredth anniversary of Emancipation, James Baldwin wrote concerning white people:

The really terrible thing, old buddy, is that *you* must accept *them*. And I mean that very seriously. You must accept them and accept them with love. For these innocent people have no other hope. They are, in effect, still trapped in a history which they do not understand; and until they understand it, they cannot be released from it. They have had to believe for many years, and for innumerable reasons, that black men are inferior to white men. Many of them, indeed, know better, but, as you will discover, people find it very difficult to act on what they know. To act is to be committed, and to be committed is to be in danger. In this case, the danger, in the minds of most white Americans, is the loss of their identity. . . . But these men are your brothers—your lost, younger brothers. And if the word *integration* means anything, this is what it means: that we, with love, shall force our brothers to see themselves as they are, to cease fleeing from reality and begin to change it.[6]

The problem with hatred and violence is that they intensify the fears of the white majority, and leave them less ashamed of their prejudices toward Negroes. In the guilt and confusion confronting our society, violence only adds to the chaos. It deepens the brutality of the oppressor and increases the bitterness of the oppressed. Violence is the antithesis of creativity and wholeness. It destroys community and makes brotherhood impossible.

My friend John Killens recently wrote in the *Negro Digest:* "Integration comes after liberation. A slave cannot integrate with his master. In the whole history of revolts and revolutions, integration has never been the main slogan of the revolution. The oppressed fights to free himself from his oppressor, not to integrate with him. Integration is the step after freedom when the freedman makes up his mind as to whether he wishes to integrate with his former master."[7]

At first glance this sounds very good. But after reflection one has to face some inescapable facts about the Negro and American life. This is a multiracial nation where all groups are dependent on each other, whether they want to recognize it or not. In this vast interdependent nation no racial group can retreat to an island entire of itself. The phenomena of integration and liberation cannot be as neatly divided as Killens would have it.

There is no theoretical or sociological divorce between liberation and integration. In our kind of society liberation cannot come without integration and integration cannot come without liberation. I speak here of integration in both the ethical and the political senses. On the one hand, integration is true intergroup, interpersonal living. On the other hand, it is the mutual sharing of power. I cannot see how the Negro will be totally liberated from the crushing weight of poor education, squalid housing and economic strangulation until he is integrated, with power, into every level of American life.

Mr. Killens's assertion might have some validity in a struggle for independence against a foreign invader. But the Negro's struggle in America is quite different from and more difficult than the struggle for independence. The American Negro will be living tomorrow with the very people against whom he is struggling today. The American Negro is not in a Congo where the Belgians will go back to Belgium after the battle is over, or in an India where the British will go back to England after independence is won. In the struggle for national independence one can talk about liberation now and integration later, but in the struggle for racial justice in a multiracial society where the oppressor and the oppressed are both "at home," liberation must come through integration.

Are we seeking power for power's sake? Or are we seeking to make the world and our nation better places to live. If we seek the latter, violence can never provide the answer. The ultimate weakness of violence is that it is a descending spiral, begetting the very thing it seeks to destroy. Instead of diminishing evil, it multiplies it. Through violence you may murder the liar, but you cannot murder the lie, nor establish the truth. Through violence you may murder the hater, but you do not murder hate. In fact, violence merely increases hate. So it goes. Returning violence for violence multiplies violence, adding deeper darkness to a night already devoid of stars. Darkness cannot drive out darkness: only light can do that. Hate cannot drive out hate: only love can do that.

The beauty of nonviolence is that in its own way and in its own time it seeks to break the chain reaction of evil. With a majestic sense of spiritual power, it seeks to elevate truth, beauty and goodness to the throne. Therefore I will continue to follow this method because I think it is the most practically sound and morally excellent way for the Negro to achieve freedom.

IV

In recent months several people have said to me: "Since violence is the new cry, isn't there a danger that you will lose touch with the people in the ghetto and be out of step with the times if you don't change your views on nonviolence?"

My answer is always the same. While I am convinced the vast majority of Negroes reject violence, even if they did not I would not be interested in being a consensus leader. I refuse to determine what is right by taking a Gallup poll of the trends of the time. I imagine that there were leaders in Germany who sincerely opposed what Hitler was doing to the Jews. But they took their poll and discovered that anti-Semitism was the prevailing trend. In order to "be in step with the times," in order to "keep in touch," they yielded to one of the most ignominious evils that history has ever known.

Ultimately a genuine leader is not a searcher for consensus but a molder of consensus. I said on one occasion, "If every Negro in the United States turns to violence, I will choose to be that one lone voice preaching that this is the wrong way." Maybe this sounded like arrogance. But it was not intended that way. It was simply my way of saying that

I would rather be a man of conviction than a man of conformity. Occasionally in life one develops a conviction so precious and meaningful that he will stand on it till the end. This is what I have found in nonviolence.

One of the greatest paradoxes of the Black Power movement is that it talks unceasingly about not imitating the values of white society, but in advocating violence it is imitating the worst, the most brutal and the most uncivilized value of American life. American Negroes have not been mass murderers. They have not murdered children in Sunday school, nor have they hung white men on trees bearing strange fruit. They have not been hooded perpetrators of violence, lynching human beings at will and drowning them at whim.

This is not to imply that the Negro is a saint who abhors violence. Unfortunately, a check of the hospitals in any Negro community on any Saturday night will make you painfully aware of the violence within the Negro community. By turning his hostility and frustration with the larger society inward, the Negro often inflicts terrible acts of violence on his own black brother. This tragic problem must be solved. But I would not advise Negroes to solve the problem by turning these inner hostilities outward through the murdering of whites. This would substitute one evil for another. Nonviolence provides a healthy way to deal with understandable anger.

I am concerned that Negroes achieve full status as citizens and as human beings here in the United States. But I am also concerned about our moral uprightness and the health of our souls. Therefore I must oppose any attempt to gain our freedom by the methods of malice, hate and violence that have characterized our oppressors. Hate is just as injurious to the hater as it is to the hated. Like an unchecked cancer, hate corrodes the personality and eats away its vital unity. Many of our inner conflicts are rooted in hate. This is why the psychiatrists say, "Love or perish." I have seen hate expressed in the countenances of too many Mississippi and Alabama sheriffs to advise the Negro to sink to this miserable level. Hate is too great a burden to bear.

Of course, you may say, this is not *practical;* life is a matter of getting even, of hitting back, of dog eat dog. Maybe in some distant Utopia, you say, that idea will work, but not in the hard, cold world in which we live. My only answer is that mankind has followed the so-called practical way for a long time now, and it has led inexorably to deeper confusion and chaos. Time is cluttered with the wreckage of individuals and communities that surrendered to hatred and violence. For the salvation of our nation and the salvation of mankind, we must follow another way. This does not mean that we abandon our militant efforts. With every ounce of our energy we must continue to rid our nation of the incubus of racial injustice. But we need not in the process relinquish our privilege and obligation to love.

Fanon says at the end of *The Wretched of the Earth:*

So, comrades, let us not pay tribute to Europe by creating states, institutions and societies which draw their inspiration from her.

Humanity is waiting for something other from us than such an imitation, which would be almost an obscene caricature.

If we want to turn Africa into a new Europe, and America into a new Europe, then let us leave the destiny of our countries to Europeans. They will know how to do it better than the most gifted among us.

But if we want humanity to advance a step further, if we want to bring it up to a different level than that which Europe has shown it, then we must invent and we must make discoveries.

If we wish to live up to our peoples' expectations, we must seek the response elsewhere than in Europe.

Moreover, if we wish to reply to the expectations of the people of Europe, it is no good sending them back a reflection, even an ideal reflection, of their society and their thought with which from time to time they feel immeasurably sickened.

For Europe, for ourselves and for humanity, comrades, we must turn over a new leaf, we must work out new concepts, and try to set afoot a new man.[8]

These are brave and challenging words; I am happy that young black men and women are quoting them. But the problem is that Fanon and those who quote his words are seeking "to work out new concepts" and "set afoot a new man" with a willingness to imitate old concepts of violence. Is there not a basic contradiction here? Violence has been the inseparable twin of materialism, the hallmark of its grandeur and misery. This is the one thing about modern civilization that I do not care to imitate.

Humanity is waiting for something other than blind imitation of the past. If we want truly to advance a step further, if we want to turn over a new leaf and really set a new man afoot, we must begin to turn mankind away from the long and desolate night of violence. May it not be that the new man the world needs is the nonviolent man? Longfellow said, "In this world a man must either be an anvil or a hammer." We must be hammers shaping a new society rather than anvils molded by the old. This not only will make us new men, but will give us a new kind of power. It will not be Lord Acton's image of power that tends to corrupt or

absolute power that corrupts absolutely. It will be power infused with love and justice, that will change dark yesterdays
into bright tomorrows, and lift us from the fatigue of despair
to the buoyancy of hope. A dark, desperate, confused and
sin-sick world waits for this new kind of man and this new
kind of power.

III

Racism and the White Backlash

I

I
t is time for all of us to tell each other the truth about who and what have brought the Negro to the condition of deprivation against which he struggles today. In human relations the truth is hard to come by, because most groups are deceived about themselves. Rationalization and the incessant search for scapegoats are the psychological cataracts that blind us to our individual and collective sins. But the day has passed for bland euphemisms. He who lives with untruth lives in spiritual slavery. Freedom is still the bonus we receive for knowing the truth. "Ye shall know the truth, and the truth shall set you free."

It would be neither true nor honest to say that the Negro's status is what it is because he is innately inferior or because he is basically lazy and listless or because he has not sought to lift himself by his own bootstraps. To find the origins of the Negro problem we must turn to the white man's problem. As Earl Conrad says in a recent book, *The Invention of the Negro:* "I have sought out these new routes in the unshakable conviction that the question involved there cannot be and never could be answered merely by examining the Negro himself, his ghettos, his history, his personality, his culture. For the answer to how the Negro's status came to be what it is does not lie essentially in the world of the Negro, but in the world of the white."[1] In short, white America must assume the guilt for the black man's inferior status.

Ever since the birth of our nation, white America has had a schizophrenic personality on the question of race. She has been torn between selves—a self in which she proudly professed the great principles of democracy and a self in which she sadly practiced the antithesis of democracy. This tragic duality has produced a strange indecisiveness and ambivalence toward the Negro, causing America to take a step backward simultaneously with every step forward on the question of racial justice, to be at once attracted to the Negro and repelled by him, to love and to hate him. There has never been a solid, unified and determined thrust to make justice a reality for Afro-Americans.

The step backward has a new name today. It is called the "white backlash." But the white backlash is nothing new. It is the surfacing of old prejudices, hostilities and ambivalences that have always been there. It was caused neither by the cry of Black Power nor by the unfortunate recent wave of riots in our cities. The white backlash of today is rooted in the same problem that has characterized America ever since the black man landed in chains on the shores of this nation. The white backlash is an expression of the same vacillations, the same search for rationalizations, the same lack of commitment that have always characterized white America on the question of race.

What is the source of this perennial indecision and vacillation? It lies in the "congenital deformity" of racism that has crippled the nation from its inception. The roots of racism are very deep in America. Historically it was so acceptable in the national life that today it still only lightly burdens the conscience. No one surveying the moral landscape of our nation can overlook the hideous and pathetic wreckage of commitment twisted and turned to a thousand shapes under the stress of prejudice and irrationality.

This does not imply that all white Americans are racists—far from it. Many white people have, through a deep moral compulsion, fought long and hard for racial justice. Nor does it mean that America has made no progress in her attempt to cure the body politic of the disease of racism, or that the dogma of racism has not been considerably modified in recent years. However, for the good of America, it is necessary to refute the idea that the dominant ideology in our country even today is freedom and equality while racism is just an occasional departure from the norm on the part of a few bigoted extremists.

What is racism? Dr. George Kelsey, in a profound book entitled *Racism and the Christian Understanding of Man,* states that

> Racism is a faith. It is a form of idolatry. . . . In its early modern beginnings, racism was a justificatory device. It did not emerge as a faith. It arose as an ideological justification for the constellations of political and economic power which were expressed in colonialism and slavery. But gradually the idea of the superior race was heightened and deepened in meaning and value so that it pointed beyond the historical structures of relation, in which it emerged, to human existence itself.[2]

In her *Race: Science and Politics,* Ruth Benedict expands on the theme by defining racism as "the dogma that one ethnic group is condemned by nature to hereditary inferiority and another group is destined to hereditary superiority. It is the dogma that the hope of civilization depends upon eliminating some races and keeping others pure. It is the dogma that one race has carried progress throughout human history and can alone ensure future progress."[3]

Since racism is based on the dogma "that the hope of civilization depends upon eliminating some races and keeping others pure," its ultimate logic is genocide. Hitler, in his mad and ruthless attempt to exterminate the Jews, carried the logic of racism to its ultimate tragic conclusions. While America has not literally sought to eliminate the Negro in this final sense, it has, through the system of segregation, substituted a subtle reduction of life by means of deprivation.

If a man asserts that another man, because of his race, is not good enough to have a job equal to his, or to eat at a lunch counter next to him, or to have access to certain hotels, or to attend school with him, or to live next door to him, he is by implication affirming that that man does not deserve to exist. He does not deserve to exist because his existence is corrupt and defective.

Racism is a philosophy based on a contempt for life. It is the arrogant assertion that one race is the center of value and object of devotion, before which other races must kneel in submission. It is the absurd dogma that one race is responsible for all the progress of history and alone can assure the progress of the future. Racism is total estrangement. It separates not only bodies, but minds and spirits. Inevitably it descends to inflicting spiritual or physical homicide upon the out-group.

Of the two dominant and contradictory strains in the American psyche, the positive one, our democratic heritage, was the later development on the American continent. Democracy, born in the eighteenth century, took from John Locke of England the theory of natural rights and the justification of revolution and imbued it with the ideal of a society governed by the people. When Jefferson wrote the Declaration of Independence, the first government of the world to be based on these principles was established on American soil. A contemporary description of Benjamin Franklin might have described the new nation: "He has torn lightning from the sky; soon he will tear their sceptres from the kings." And Thomas Paine in his enthusiasm declared, "We have the power to begin the world over again."

Yet even amid these electrifying expressions of the rights of man, racism—the myth of inferior peoples—was flourishing here to contradict and qualify the democratic ideal. Slavery was not only ignored in defining democracy, but its enlargement was tolerated in the interests of strengthening the nation.

For more than two hundred years before the Declaration of Independence, Africa had been raped and plundered by Britain and Europe, her native kingdoms disorganized, and her people and rulers demoralized. For a hundred years afterward, the infamous trade continued in America virtually without abatement, even after it had ceased to be legal on this continent.

In fact, this ghastly blood traffic was so immense and its profits were so stupendous that the economies of several European nations owed their growth and prosperity to it and New England rested heavily on it for its development. [Charles A.] Beard declared it was fair to say of whole towns in New England and Great Britain: "The stones of your houses are cemented with the blood of African slaves." Conservatively estimated, several million Africans died in the calloused transfer of human merchandise to the New World alone.

It is important to understand that the basis for the birth,

growth and development of slavery in America was primarily economic. By the beginning of the seventeenth century, the British Empire had established colonies all along the Atlantic seaboard, from Massachusetts to the West Indies, to serve as producers of raw materials for British manufacturing, a market for goods manufactured in Britain and a source of staple cargoes for British shipping engaged in world trade. So the colonies had to provide an abundance of rice, sugar, cotton and tobacco. In the first few years of the various settlements along the East Coast, so-called indentured servants, mostly white, were employed on plantations. But within a generation the plantation operators were demanding outright and lifetime slavery for the Africans they imported. As a function of this new economic policy, Africans were reduced to the status of property by law, and this status was enforced by the most rigid and brutal police power of the existing governments. By 1650 slavery had been legally established as a national institution.

Since the institution of slavery was so important to the economic development of America, it had a profound impact in shaping the social-political-legal structure of the nation. Land and slaves were the chief forms of private property, property was wealth and the voice of wealth made the law and determined politics. In the service of this system, human beings were reduced to propertyless property. Black men, the creators of the wealth of the New World, were stripped of all human and civil rights. And this degradation was sanctioned and protected by institutions of government, all for one purpose: to produce commodities for sale at a profit, which in turn would be privately appropriated.

It seems to be a fact of life that human beings cannot continue to do wrong without eventually reaching out for some rationalization to clothe their acts in the garments of righteousness. And so, with the growth of slavery, men had to convince themselves that a system which was so economically profitable was morally justifiable. The attempt to give moral sanction to a profitable system gave birth to the doctrine of white supremacy.

Religion and the Bible were cited and distorted to support the status quo. It was argued that the Negro was inferior by nature because of Noah's curse upon the children of Ham. The Apostle Paul's dictum became a watchword: "Servant, be obedient to your master." In this strange way theology became a ready ally of commerce. The great Puritan divine Cotton Mather culled the Bible for passages to give comfort to the plantation owners and merchants. He went so far as to set up some "Rules for the Society of Negroes," in which, among other things, Negroes disobedient to their masters were to be rebuked and denied attendance at church meetings, and runaway slaves were to be brought back and severely punished. All of this, he reasoned, was in line with the Apostle Paul's injunction that servants should be obedient to their masters.

Logic was manipulated to give intellectual credence to the system of slavery. Someone formulated the argument for the inferiority of the Negro in the shape of a syllogism:

All men are made in the image of God;
God, as everybody knows, is not a Negro;
Therefore the Negro is not a man.

Academicians eventually climbed on the bandwagon and gave their prestige to the myth of the superior race. Their contribution came through the so-called Teutonic Origins theory, a doctrine of white supremacy surrounded by the halo of academic respectability. The theorists of this concept argued that all Anglo-Saxon institutions of any worth had their historical roots in the Teutonic tribal institutions of ancient Germany, and furthermore that "only the Teutonic race had been imbued with the ability to build stable governments." Historians from the lofty academic towers of Oxford, like Bishop William Stubbs and Edward A. Freeman, expounded the Teutonic Origins theory in British intellectual circles. It leaped the Atlantic and found lodging in the mind of Herbert Baxter Adams, one of the organizers of the graduate school at Johns Hopkins University and founder of the American Historical Association. He expanded Freeman's views by asserting that the Teutonic Origins theory really had "three homes—England, Germany and the United States." Pretty soon this distorted theory dominated the thinking of American historians at leading universities like Harvard, Cornell, Wisconsin and Columbia.

Even natural science, that discipline committed to the inductive method, creative appraisal and detached objectivity, was invoked and distorted to give credence to a political position. A whole school of racial ethnologists developed using such terms as "species," "genus" and "race." It became fashionable to think of the slave as a "species of property." It was during this period that the word "race" came into fashion.

Dr. Samuel G. Morton, a Philadelphia physician, emerged with the head-size theory which affirmed that the larger the skull, the superior the individual. This theory was used by other ethnologists to prove that the large head size of Caucasians signified more intellectual capacity and more native worth. A Dr. Josiah C. Nott, in his *Collections on the Natural History of the Caucasian and Negro Races,* used pseudoscientific evidence to prove that the black man was little above the level of an ape. A Frenchman, Count Arthur de Gobineau, in his book *The Inequality of the Human Races,* vigorously defended the theory of the inferiority of the black man and used the experience of the United States as his prime source of evidence. It was this kind of "science" that pervaded the atmosphere in the nineteenth century, and these pseudo-scientists became the authoritative references for any and all seeking rationalization for the system of slavery.

Generally we think of white supremacist views as having their origins with the unlettered, underprivileged, poorer-class whites. But the social obstetricians who presided at the birth of racist views in our country were from the aristocracy: rich merchants, influential clergymen, men of medical science, historians and political scientists from some of the leading universities of the nation. With such a distinguished company of the elite working so assiduously to disseminate racist views, what was there to inspire poor, illiterate, unskilled white farmers to think otherwise?

Soon the doctrine of white supremacy was imbedded in every textbook and preached in practically every pulpit. It became a structural part of the culture. And men then embraced this philosophy, not as the rationalization of a lie, but as the expression of a final truth. In 1857 the system of slavery was given its ultimate legal support by the Supreme Court of the United States in the Dred Scott decision, which affirmed that the Negro had no rights that the white man was bound to respect.

The greatest blasphemy of the whole ugly process was that the white man ended up making God his partner in the exploitation of the Negro. What greater heresy has religion known? Ethical Christianity vanished and the moral nerve of religion was atrophied. This terrible distortion sullied the essential nature of Christianity.

Virtually all of the Founding Fathers of our nation, even those who rose to the heights of the presidency, those whom

we cherish as our authentic heroes, were so enmeshed in
the ethos of slavery and white supremacy that not one ever
emerged with a clear, unambiguous stand on Negro rights.
No human being is perfect. In our individual and collective lives every expression of greatness is followed, not by a
period symbolizing completeness, but by a comma implying
partialness. Following every affirmation of greatness is the
conjunction "but." Naaman "was a great man," says the Old
Testament, "but . . ."—that "but" reveals something tragic
and disturbing—"but he was a leper." George Washington,
Thomas Jefferson, Patrick Henry, John Quincy Adams, John
Calhoun and Abraham Lincoln were great men, but—that
"but" underscores the fact that not one of these men had a
strong, unequivocal belief in the equality of the black man.

No one doubts the valor and commitment that characterized George Washington's life. But to the end of his days
he maintained a posture of exclusionism toward the slave.
He was a fourth-generation slaveholder. He only allowed
Negroes to enter the Continental Army because His Majes-
ty's Crown was attempting to recruit Negroes to the British
cause. Washington was not without his moments of torment, those moments of conscience when something within
told him that slavery was wrong. As he searched the future
of America one day, he wrote to his nephew: "I wish from
my soul that the legislature of this State could see the policy
of gradual abolition of slavery. It might prevent much future
mischief." In spite of this, Washington never made a public
statement condemning slavery. He could not pull away from
the system. When he died he owned, or had on lease, more
than 160 slaves.

Here, in the life of the father of our nation, we can see
the developing dilemma of white America: the haunting am-

bivalence, the intellectual and moral recognition that slavery is wrong, but the emotional tie to the system so deep and pervasive that it imposes an inflexible unwillingness to root it out.

Thomas Jefferson reveals the same ambivalence. There is much in the life of Jefferson that can serve as a model for political leaders in every age; he came close to the ideal "philosopher-king" that Plato dreamed of centuries ago. But in spite of this, Jefferson was a child of his culture who had been influenced by the pseudoscientific and philosophical thought that rationalized slavery. In his *Notes on Virginia,* Jefferson portrayed the Negro as inferior to the white man in his endowments of body, mind and imagination, although he observed that the Negro appeared to be superior at picking out tunes on the "banjar." Jefferson's majestic words, "all men are created equal," meant for him, as for many others, that all *white* men are created equal.

Yet in his heart Jefferson knew that slavery was wrong and that it degraded the white man's mind and soul. In the same *Notes on Virginia* he wrote: "For if a slave can have a country in this world, it must be any other in preference to that in which he is born to live and labor for another. . . . Indeed I tremble for my country when I reflect that God is just, that his justice cannot sleep forever . . . the Almighty has no attribute which can take sides with us in such a contest." And in 1820, six years before his death, he wrote these melancholy words: "But the momentous question [slavery] like a fire-bell in the night, awakened and filled me with terror. I considered it at once as the knell of the Union. . . . I regret that I am now to die in the belief that the useless sacrifice of themselves by the generation of 1776, to acquire self-government and happiness to their country, is to be thrown away by the unwise and unworthy passion of their sons, and that my only consolation is to be that I live not to weep over it."

This strange duality toward the Negro and slavery vexed the mind of Abraham Lincoln for years. Few men in history have anchored their lives more deeply in moral convictions than Abraham Lincoln, but on the question of slavery Lincoln's torments and vacillations were tenacious.

As early as 1837, as a state legislator, Lincoln referred to the injustice and impracticality of slavery. Later he wrote of the physical differences between blacks and whites and made it clear that he felt whites were superior. At times he concluded that the white man could not live with the Negro. This accounted for his conviction that the only answer to the problem was to colonize the black man—send him back to Africa, or to the West Indies or some other isolated spot. This view was still in his mind toward the height of the Civil War. Delegation after delegation—the Quakers above all, great abolitionists like Charles Sumner, Horace Greeley and William Lloyd Garrison—pleaded with Lincoln to free the slaves, but he was firm in his resistance. Frederick Douglass, a Negro of towering grandeur, sound judgment and militant initiative, sought, without success, to persuade Lincoln that slavery, not merely the preservation of the union, was at the root of the war. At the time, Lincoln could not yet see it.

A civil war raged within Lincoln's own soul, a tension between the Dr. Jekyll of freedom and the Mr. Hyde of slavery, a struggle like that of Plato's charioteer with two head-strong horses each pulling in different directions. Morally Lincoln was for black emancipation, but emotionally, like most of his white contemporaries, he was for a long time unable to act in accordance with his conscience.

But Lincoln was basically honest and willing to admit his confusions. He saw that the nation could not survive half slave and half free; and he said, "If we could first know where we are and whither we are tending, we could better judge what to do and how to do it." Fortunately for the nation, he finally came to see "whither we were tending." On January 1, 1863, he issued the Emancipation Proclamation, freeing the Negro from the bondage of chattel slavery. By this concrete act of courage his reservations of the past were overshadowed. The conclusion of his search is embodied in these words: "In giving freedom to the slave, we assure freedom to the free,—honourable alike is what we give and what we preserve."

The significance of the Emancipation Proclamation was described by Frederick Douglass in these words:

Unquestionably, for weal or for woe, the First of January is to be the most memorable day in American Annals. The Fourth of July was great, but the First of January, when we consider it in all its relations and bearings, is incomparably greater. The one had respect to the mere political birth of a nation; the last concerns the national life and character, and is to determine whether that life and character shall be radiantly glorious with all high and noble virtues, or infamously blackened, forevermore.[4]

But underneath, the ambivalence of white America toward the Negro still lurked with painful persistence. With all the beautiful promise that Douglass saw in the Emancipation Proclamation, he soon found that it left the Negro with only abstract freedom. Four million newly liberated slaves found themselves with no bread to eat, no land to cultivate, no shelter to cover their heads. It was like freeing a man who had been unjustly imprisoned for years, and on discovering his innocence sending him out with no bus fare to get home, no suit to cover his body, no financial compensation to atone for his long years of incarceration and to help him get a sound footing in society; sending him out with only the assertion: "Now you are free." What greater injustice could society perpetrate? All the moral voices of the universe, all the codes of sound jurisprudence, would rise up with condemnation at such an act. Yet this is exactly what America did to the Negro. In 1863 the Negro was given abstract freedom expressed in luminous rhetoric. But in an agrarian economy he was given no land to make liberation concrete. After the war the government granted white settlers, without cost, millions of acres of land in the West, thus providing America's new white peasants from Europe with an economic floor. But at the same time its oldest peasantry, the Negro, was denied everything but a legal status he could not use, could not consolidate, could not even defend. As Frederick Douglass came to say, "Emancipation granted the Negro freedom to hunger, freedom to winter amid the rains of heaven. Emancipation was freedom and famine at the same time."

The inscription on the Statue of Liberty refers to America as the "mother of exiles." The tragedy is that while America became the mother of her white exiles, she evinced no motherly concern or love for her exiles from Africa. It is no wonder that out of despair and estrangement the Negro cries out in one of his sorrow songs: "Sometimes I feel like a motherless child." The marvel is, as Frederick Douglass once said, that Negroes are still alive.

In dealing with the ambivalence of white America, we must not overlook another form of racism that was relentlessly pursued on American shores: the physical extermination of the American Indian. The South American example of absorbing the indigenous Indian population was ignored in the United States, and systematic destruction of a whole people was undertaken. The common phrase, "The only good Indian is a dead Indian," was virtually elevated to national policy. Thus the poisoning of the American mind was accomplished not only by acts of discrimination and exploitation but by the exaltation of murder as an expression of the courage and initiative of the pioneer. Just as Southern culture was made to appear noble by ignoring the cruelty of slavery, the conquest of the Indian was depicted as an example of bravery and progress.

Thus through two centuries a continuous indoctrination of Americans has separated people according to mythically superior and inferior qualities while a democratic spirit of equality was evoked as the national ideal. These concepts of racism, and this schizophrenic duality of conduct, remain deeply rooted in American thought today. This tendency of the nation to take one step forward on the question of racial justice and then to take a step backward is still the pattern. Just as an ambivalent nation freed the slaves a century ago with no plan or program to make their freedom meaningful, the still ambivalent nation in 1954 declared school segregation unconstitutional with no plan or program to make integration real. Just as the Congress passed a civil rights bill in 1868 and refused to enforce it, the Congress passed a civil rights bill in 1964 and to this day has failed to enforce it in all its dimensions. Just as the Fifteenth Amendment in 1870 proclaimed Negro suffrage, only to permit its de facto withdrawal in half the nation, so in 1965 the Voting Rights Law was passed and then permitted to languish with only fractional and halfhearted implementation.

The civil rights measures of the 1960s engraved solemn

rights in the legal literature. But after writing piecemeal and incomplete legislation and proclaiming its historic importance in magnificent prose, the American government left the Negro to make the unworkable work. Against entrenched segregationist state power, with almost total dependence economically on those they had to contend with, and without political experience, the impoverished Negro was expected to usher in an era of freedom and plenty.

When the war against poverty came into being in 1964, it seemed to herald a new day of compassion. It was the bold assertion that the nation would no longer stand complacently by while millions of its citizens smothered in poverty in the midst of opulence. But it did not take long to discover that the government was only willing to appropriate such a limited budget that it could not launch a good skirmish against poverty, much less a full-scale war.

Moreover, the poverty program, which in concept elated the Negro poor, became so embroiled in political turmoil that its insufficiencies were magnified and its operations paralyzed. Big-city machines felt threatened by it and small towns, especially in the South, directed it away from Negroes. Its good intentions and limited objectives were frustrated by the skillful maneuvers of experienced politicians. The worst effect of these manipulations was to cast doubt upon the program as a whole and discredit those Negroes involved directly in its administration.

In 1965 the President presented a new plan to Congress —which it finally passed in 1966—for rebuilding entire slum neighborhoods. With other elements of the program it would, in his words, make the decaying cities of the present into "the masterpieces of our civilization." This Demonstration Cities plan is imaginative; it embodies social vision and properly defines racial discrimination as a central evil.

However, the ordinary Negro, though no social or political analyst, will be skeptical. He will be skeptical, first, because of the insufficient funds assigned to the program. He will be skeptical, second, because he knows how many laws exist in Northern states and cities prohibiting discrimination in housing, in education and in employment; he knows how many overlapping commissions exist to enforce the terms of these laws—and he knows how he lives. The ubiquitous discrimination in his daily life tells him that laws on paper, no matter how imposing their terms, will not guarantee that he will live in "the masterpiece of civilization."

Throughout our history, laws affirming Negro rights have consistently been circumvented by ingenious evasions which render them void in practice. Laws that affect the whole population—draft laws, income-tax laws, traffic laws—manage to work even though they may be unpopular; but laws passed for the Negro's benefit are so widely unenforced that it is a mockery to call them laws. There is a tragic gulf between civil rights laws passed and civil rights laws implemented. There is a double standard in the enforcement of law and a double standard in the respect for particular laws.

All of this tells us that the white backlash is nothing new. White America has been backlashing on the fundamental God-given and human rights of Negro Americans for more than three hundred years. With all of her dazzling achievements and stupendous material strides, America has maintained its strange ambivalence on the question of racial justice.

II

To define much of white America as self-deluded on the commitment to equality and to apprehend the broad base on which it rests are not to enthrone pessimism. The racism of

today is real, but the democratic spirit that has always faced
it is equally real. The value in pulling racism out of its ob-
scurity and stripping it of its rationalizations lies in the confidence that it can be changed. To live with the pretense that
racism is a doctrine of a very few is to disarm us in fighting
it frontally as scientifically unsound, morally repugnant and
socially destructive. The prescription for the cure rests with
the accurate diagnosis of the disease. A people who began a
national life inspired by a vision of a society of brotherhood
can redeem itself. But redemption can come only through a
humble acknowledgment of guilt and an honest knowledge
of self.

Jesus once told a parable of a young man who left home
and wandered into a far country, where he sought life in
adventure after adventure. But he found only frustration and
bewilderment. The farther he moved from his father's house,
the closer he came to the house of despair. After the boy had
wasted all, a famine developed in the land, and he ended up
seeking food in a pig's trough. But the story does not end
here. In a state of disillusionment, frustration and homesick-
ness, the boy "came to himself" and said, "I will arise and go
to my father, and will say unto him, Father, I have sinned
against heaven, and before thee." The prodigal son was not
himself when he left his father's house or when he dreamed
that pleasure was the end of life. Only when he made up his
mind to go home and be a son again did he come to himself.
The boy returned home to find a loving father waiting with
outstretched arms and a heart filled with joy.

This is an analogy to what white America confronts today. Like all human analogies, it is imperfect, but it does suggest some parallels worth considering. America has strayed
to the far country of racism. The home that all too many

Americans left was solidly structured idealistically. Its pillars were soundly grounded in the insights of our Judeo-Christian heritage: all men are made in the image of God; all men are brothers; all men are created equal; every man is heir to a legacy of dignity and worth; every man has rights that are neither conferred by nor derived from the state, they are God-given. What a marvelous foundation for any home! What a glorious place to inhabit! But America strayed away; and this excursion has brought only confusion and bewilderment. It has left hearts aching with guilt and minds distorted with irrationality. It has driven wisdom from the throne. This long and callous sojourn in the far country of racism has brought a moral and spiritual famine to the nation.

But it is not too late to return home. If America would come to herself and return to her true home, "one nation, indivisible, with liberty and justice for all," she would give the democratic creed a new authentic ring, enkindle the imagination of mankind and fire the souls of men. If she fails, she will be victimized with the ultimate social psychosis that can lead only to national suicide.

In 1944 Gunnar Myrdal, the Swedish economist, wrote in *An American Dilemma*:

> The Negro problem is not only America's greatest failure but also America's incomparably great opportunity for the future. If America should follow its own deepest convictions, its well-being at home would be increased directly. At the same time America's prestige and power abroad would rise immensely. The century-old dream of American patriots, that America should give to the entire world its own freedoms and its own faith, would come true. America can demon-

strate that justice, equality and cooperation are possible between white and colored people. .... *America
is free to choose whether the Negro shall remain her liability
or become her opportunity.*[5]

This is white America's most urgent challenge today. If
America is to respond creatively to the challenge, many individuals, groups and agencies must rise above the hypocrisies
of the past and begin to take an immediate and determined
part in changing the face of their nation. If the country has
not yet emerged with a massive program to end the blight
surrounding the life of the Negro, one is forced to believe
that the answers have not been forthcoming because there is
as yet no genuine and widespread conviction that such fundamental changes are needed, and needed now.

As a first step on the journey home, the journey to full
equality, we will have to engage in a radical reordering of
national priorities. As the *Carnegie Quarterly* declares: "A
great deal of money is spent in this country every day, for
education and for housing, freeways, war, national parks, li-
quor, cosmetics, advertising and a lot of other things. It is a
question of the allocation of money, which means the establishing of priorities."[6]

Are we more concerned with the size, power and wealth
of our society or with creating a more just society? The failure to pursue justice is not only a moral default. Without it
social tensions will grow and the turbulence in the streets will
persist despite disapproval or repressive action. Even more,
a withered sense of justice in an expanding society leads to
corruption of the lives of all Americans. All too many of
those who live in affluent America ignore those who exist
in poor America; in doing so, the affluent Americans will

eventually have to face themselves with the question that Eichmann chose to ignore: how responsible am I for the well-being of my fellows? To ignore evil is to become an accomplice to it.

Today the exploration of space is engaging not only our enthusiasm but our patriotism. Developing it as a global race we have intensified its inherent drama and brought its adventure into every living room, nursery, shop and office. No such fervor or exhilaration attends the war on poverty. There is impatience with its problems, indifference toward its progress and hostility toward its errors. Without denying the value of scientific endeavor, there is a striking absurdity in committing billions to reach the moon where no people live, while only a fraction of that amount is appropriated to service the densely populated slums. If these strange values persist, in a few years we can be assured that when we set a man on the moon, with an adequate telescope he will be able to see the slums on earth with their intensified congestion, decay and turbulence. On what scale of values is this a program of progress?

In the wasteland of war, the expenditure of resources knows no restraints; here our abundance is fully recognized and enthusiastically squandered. The recently revealed misestimate of the war budget amounts to $10 billion for a single year. The error alone is more than five times the amount committed to antipoverty programs. If we reversed investments and gave the armed forces the antipoverty budget, the generals could be forgiven if they walked off the battlefield in disgust. The *Washington Post* has calculated that we spend $332,000 for each enemy we kill. It challenges the imagination to contemplate what lives we could transform if we were to cease killing. The security we profess to seek in foreign adventures we will lose in our decaying cities. The bombs in Vietnam explode at home; they destroy the hopes and possibilities for a decent America.

A considerable part of the Negro's efforts of the past decades has been devoted, particularly in the South, to attaining a sense of dignity. For us, enduring the sacrifices of beatings, jailings and even death was acceptable merely to have access to public accommodations. To sit at a lunch counter or occupy the front seat of a bus had no effect on our material standard of living, but in removing a caste stigma it revolutionized our psychology and elevated the spiritual content of our being. Instinctively we struck out for dignity first because personal degradation as an inferior human being was even more keenly felt than material privation.

But dignity is also corroded by poverty no matter how poetically we invest the humble with simple graces and charm. No worker can maintain his morale or sustain his spirit if in the market place his capacities are declared to be worthless to society. The Negro is no longer ashamed that he is black— he should never have permitted himself to accept the absurd concept that white is more virtuous than black, but he was crushed by the propaganda that superiority had a pale countenance. That day is fast coming to an end. However, in his search for human dignity he is handicapped by the stigma of poverty in a society whose measure of value revolves about money. If the society changes its concepts by placing the responsibility on its system, not on the individual, and guarantees secure employment or a minimum income, dignity will come within reach of all. For Negroes, the goal on which they have placed the highest priority, which the emancipation from slavery was intended to assure, will finally be attained.

Meanwhile, any discussion of the problems of inequality

is meaningless unless a time dimension is given to programs for their solution. The Great Society is only a phrase so long as no date is set for the achievement of its promises. It is disquieting to note that President Johnson in his message to Congress on the Demonstration Cities program stated, "If we can begin now the planning from which action will flow, the hopes of the twentieth century will become the realities of the twenty-first." On this timetable many Negroes not yet born and virtually all now alive will not experience equality. The virtue of patience will become a vice if it accepts so leisurely an approach to social change.

III

A leading voice in the chorus of social transition belongs to the white liberal, whether he speak through the government, the church, the voluntary welfare agencies or the civil rights movement. Over the last few years many Negroes have felt that their most troublesome adversary was not the obvious bigot of the Ku Klux Klan or the John Birch Society, but the white liberal who is more devoted to "order" than to justice, who prefers tranquillity to equality. In a sense the white liberal has been victimized with some of the same ambivalence that has been a constant part of our national heritage. Even in areas where liberals have great influence—labor unions, schools, churches and politics—the situation of the Negro is not much better than in areas where they are not dominant. This is why many liberals have fallen into the trap of seeing integration in merely aesthetic terms, where a token number of Negroes adds color to a white-dominated power structure. They say, "Our union is integrated from top to bottom, we even have one Negro on the executive board"; or "Our neighborhood is making great progress in integrated housing, we now have two Negro families"; or

"Our university has no problem with integration, we have one Negro faculty member and even one Negro chairman of a department."

Often white liberals are unaware of their latent prejudices. A while ago I ran into a white woman who was anxious to discuss the race problem with me. She said: "I am very liberal. I have no prejudices toward Negroes. I believe Negroes should have the right to vote, the right to a good job, the right to a decent home and the right to have access to public accommodations. Of course, I must confess that I would not want my daughter to marry a Negro." This lady could not see that her failure to accept intermarriage negated her claim to genuine liberalism. She failed to see that implicit in her rejection was the feeling that her daughter had some pure, superior nature that should not be contaminated by the impure, inferior nature of the Negro. It is the Teutonic Origins theory warmed over. The question of intermarriage is never raised in a society cured of the disease of racism.

Yet in spite of this latent prejudice, in spite of the hard reality that many blatant forms of injustice could not exist without the acquiescence of white liberals, the fact remains that a sound resolution of the race problem in America will rest with those white men and women who consider themselves as generous and decent human beings. Edmund Burke said on one occasion: "When evil men combine, good men must unite." This is the pressing challenge confronting the white liberal. When evil men plot, good men must plan. When evil men burn and bomb, good men must build and bind. When evil men conspire to preserve an unjust status quo, good men must unite to bring about the birth of a society undergirded by justice. Nothing can be more detrimental to the health of America at this time than for liberals to sink into a state of apathy and indifference.

The white liberal must see that the Negro needs not only love but also justice. It is not enough to say, "We love Negroes, we have many Negro friends." They must demand justice for Negroes. Love that does not satisfy justice is no love at all. It is merely a sentimental affection, little more than what one would have for a pet. Love at its best is justice concretized. Love is unconditional. It is not conditional upon one's staying in his place or watering down his demands in order to be considered respectable. He who contends that he "used to love the Negro, but . . ." did not truly love him in the beginning, because his love was conditioned upon the Negroes' limited demands for justice.

The white liberal must affirm that absolute justice for the Negro simply means, in the Aristotelian sense, that the Negro must have "his due." There is nothing abstract about this. It is as concrete as having a good job, a good education, a decent house and a share of power. It is, however, important to understand that giving a man his due may often mean giving him special treatment. I am aware of the fact that this has been a troublesome concept for many liberals, since it conflicts with their traditional ideal of equal opportunity and equal treatment of people according to their individual merits. But this is a day which demands new thinking and the reevaluation of old concepts. A society that has done something special *against* the Negro for hundreds of years must now do something special *for* him, in order to equip him to compete on a just and equal basis.[7]

The white liberal must rid himself of the notion that there can be a tensionless transition from the old order of injustice to the new order of justice. Two things are clear to me, and I hope they are clear to white liberals. One is that the Negro cannot achieve emancipation through violent rebellion. The other is that the Negro cannot achieve emancipation by passively waiting for the white race voluntarily to grant it to him. The Negro has not gained a single right in America without persistent pressure and agitation. However lamentable it may seem, the Negro is now convinced that white America will never admit him to equal rights unless it is coerced into doing it.

Nonviolent coercion always brings tension to the surface. This tension, however, must not be seen as destructive. There is a kind of tension that is both healthy and necessary for growth. Society needs nonviolent gadflies to bring its tensions into the open and force its citizens to confront the ugliness of their prejudices and the tragedy of their racism.

It is important for the liberal to see that the oppressed person who agitates for his rights is not the creator of tension. He merely brings out the hidden tension that is already alive. Last summer when we had our open housing marches in Chicago, many of our white liberal friends cried out in horror and dismay: "You are creating hatred and hostility in the white communities in which you are marching. You are only developing a white backlash." I never could understand this logic. They failed to realize that the hatred and the hostilities were already latently or subconsciously present. Our marches merely brought them to the surface. How strange it would be to condemn a physician who, through persistent work and the ingenuity of his medical skills, discovered cancer in a patient. Would anyone be so ignorant as to say he caused the cancer? Through the skills and discipline of direct action we reveal that there is a dangerous cancer of hatred and racism in our society. We did not cause the cancer; we merely exposed it. Only through this kind of exposure will the cancer ever be cured. The committed white liberal must see the need for powerful antidotes to combat the disease of racism.

The white liberal must escalate his support for the struggle for racial justice rather than de-escalate it. This would be a tragic time to forsake and withdraw from the struggle. The need for commitment is greater today than ever. Admittedly, hostile words are being uttered by a few Negroes against all whites, and some would like to read whites out of the movement entirely. But these represent a very small minority in the Negro community. Most Negroes are still committed to the principle of white and black cooperation.

Admittedly, too, a few Negroes have uttered anti-Semitic sentiments. Because racism is a shameful evil wherever it may exist, and because among Negroes anti-Semitism is a particularly freakish phenomenon, it warrants examination.

One fact is decisive for perspective and balance: the amount of anti-Semitism found among Negroes is no greater than is found among white groups of the same economic strata. Two polls cited by Professor Thomas Pettigrew and a very recent study in depth conducted by Dr. Oscar Lewis arrive at this same conclusion. These revelations should allay the alarm that has arisen from exploitation and exaggeration of the issue by some white and Negro publicists whose appetite for attention exceeds their attachment to truth and responsibility.

The question that troubles many Jews and other concerned Americans is why oppressed Negroes should harbor any anti-Semitism at all. Prejudice and discrimination can only harm them; therefore it would appear they should be virtually immune to their sinister appeal.

The limited degree of Negro anti-Semitism is substantially a Northern ghetto phenomenon; it virtually does not exist in the South. The urban Negro has a special and unique relationship to Jews. He meets them in two dissimilar roles. On the one hand, he is associated with Jews as some of his most committed and generous partners in the civil rights struggle. On the other hand, he meets them daily as some of his most direct exploiters in the ghetto as slum landlords and gouging shopkeepers. Jews have identified with Negroes voluntarily in the freedom movement, motivated by their religious and cultural commitment to justice. The other Jews who are engaged in commerce in the ghettos are remnants of older communities. A great number of Negro ghettos were formerly Jewish neighborhoods; some storekeepers and landlords remained as population changes occurred. They operate with the ethics of marginal business entrepreneurs, not Jewish ethics, but the distinction is lost on some Negroes who are maltreated by them. Such Negroes, caught in frustration and irrational anger, parrot racial epithets. They foolishly add to the social poison that injures themselves and their own people.

It would be a tragic and immoral mistake to identify the mass of Negroes with the very small number that succumb to cheap and dishonest slogans, just as it would be a serious error to identify all Jews with the few who exploit Negroes under their economic sway.

Negroes cannot rationally expect honorable Jews to curb the few who are rapacious; they have no means of disciplining or suppressing them. We can only expect them to share our disgust and disdain. Negroes cannot be expected to curb and eliminate the few who are anti-Semitic, because they are subject to no controls we can exercise. We can, however, oppose them and have, in concrete ways. There has never been an instance of articulated Negro anti-Semitism that was not swiftly condemned by virtually all Negro leaders with the support of the overwhelming majority. I have myself directly attacked it within the Negro community, because it is wrong. I will continue to oppose it, because it is immoral and self-destructive.

History has shown that, like a virulent disease germ, racism can grow and destroy nations. Negroes, themselves grossly abused by it, have resolutely preserved a shining virtue: they have never been guilty of crimes against a whole people. I will always do everything in my power to maintain this precious distinction.

There is another mood, however, which represents a large number of Negroes. It is the feeling that Negroes must be their own spokesmen, that they must be in the primary leadership of their own organizations. White liberals must understand this. It is a part of the search for manhood. It is the psychological need for those who have had such a crushed and bruised history to feel and know that they are men, that they have the organizational ability to map their own strategy and shape their own programs, that they can develop the programs to shape their own destinies, that they can be their own spokesmen. When the Negro was completely an underdog, he needed white spokesmen. Liberals played their parts in this period exceedingly well. In assault after assault, they led the intellectual revolt against racism, and took the initiative in founding the civil rights organizations. But now that the Negro has rejected his role as the underdog, he has become more assertive in his search for identity and group solidarity; he wants to speak for himself.

This means that white liberals must be prepared to accept a transformation of their role. Whereas it was once a primary and spokesman role, it must now become a secondary and supportive role. This does not mean that whites must work only with whites and blacks with blacks; such an approach is always in danger of polarizations that can only intensify distrust and despair. Every time a Negro in the slums of Chicago or on the plantations of Mississippi sees Negroes and whites honestly working together for a common goal, he sees new grounds for hope. This is why I always have in the past and will in the future insist that my staff in SCLC be interracial. By insisting on racial openness in our organizations, we are setting a pattern for the racially integrated society toward which we work.

Therefore whites must continue to support and work in the civil rights movement. No vitriolic words on the part of some Negroes, no misguided shouts of "We don't want you," no abuse of the concept of Black Power should cause committed whites to curtail their support of civil rights. The issue is injustice and immorality. This was the issue before shouts of "Black Power" came into being and this will be the issue when the shouts die down.

During the Meredith Mississippi March, when some of the young activists were saying, "We don't want whites," Bishop Moore of the Episcopal Church said to Walter Fauntroy of the Washington office of SCLC: "I don't care what they say. That march is protesting a moral evil, an evil detrimental to me and every American. I am going down there whether they want me or not." This is a bold way of putting it, and this boldness says something to every white liberal. The white liberal must honestly ask himself why he supported the movement in the first place. If he supported it for the right reasons, he will continue to support it in spite of the confusions of the present moment. But if he supported the movement for the wrong reasons, he will find every available excuse to withdraw from it now, and he will discover that he was inoculated with so mild a form of commitment that he was immune to the genuine moral article.

As Negroes move forward toward a fundamental alteration of their lives, some bitter white opposition is bound to grow, even within groups that were hospitable to earlier superficial amelioration. Conflicts are unavoidable because a stage has been reached in which the reality of equality will require extensive adjustments in the way of life of some of the white majority. Many of our former supporters will fall by the wayside as the movement presses against financial privilege. Others will withdraw as long-established cultural privileges are threatened. During this period we will have to depend on that creative minority of true believers.

The hope of the world is still in dedicated minorities. The trailblazers in human, academic, scientific and religious freedom have always been in the minority. That creative minority of whites absolutely committed to civil rights can make it clear to the larger society that vacillation and procrastination on the question of racial justice can no longer be tolerated. It will take such a small committed minority to work unrelentingly to win the uncommitted majority. Such a group may well transform America's greatest dilemma into her most glorious opportunity.

IV

Among the forces of white liberalism the church has a special obligation. It is the voice of moral and spiritual authority on earth. Yet no one observing the history of the church in America can deny the shameful fact that it has been an accomplice in structuring racism into the architecture of American society. The church, by and large, sanctioned slavery and surrounded it with the halo of moral respectability. It also cast the mantle of its sanctity over the system of segregation. The unpardonable sin, thought the poet Milton, was when a man so repeatedly said, "Evil, be thou my good," so consistently lived a lie, that he lost the capacity to distinguish between good and evil. America's segregated churches come dangerously close to being in that position.

Of course, there have been marvelous exceptions. Over the last five years many religious bodies—Catholic, Protestant and Jewish—have been in the vanguard of the civil rights struggle, and have sought desperately to make the ethical insights of our Judeo-Christian heritage relevant on the question of race. But the church as a whole has been all too negligent on the question of civil rights. It has too often blessed a status quo that needed to be blasted, and reassured a social order that needed to be reformed. So the church must acknowledge its guilt, its weak and vacillating witness, its all too frequent failure to obey the call to servanthood. Today the judgment of God is upon the church for its failure to be true to its mission. If the church does not recapture its prophetic zeal, it will become an irrelevant social club without moral or spiritual authority.

A religion true to its mission knows that segregation is morally wrong and sinful. Segregation is established on pride, hatred and falsehood. It is unbrotherly and impersonal. Two segregated souls never meet in God. Segregation denies the sacredness of human personality.

Deeply rooted in our religious heritage is the conviction that every man is an heir to a legacy of dignity and worth. Our Judeo-Christian tradition refers to this inherent dignity of man in the Biblical term "the image of God." "The image of God" is universally shared in equal portions by all men. There is no graded scale of essential worth. Every human being has etched in his personality the indelible stamp of the Creator. Every man must be respected because God loves him. The worth of an individual does not lie in the measure of his intellect, his racial origin or his social position. Human worth lies in relatedness to God. An individual has value because he has value to God. Whenever this is recognized, "whiteness" and "blackness" pass away as determinants in a relationship and "son" and "brother" are substituted. Immanuel Kant said that "all men must be treated as *ends* and never as mere *means*." The immorality of segregation is that it treats men as means rather than ends, and thereby reduces them to things rather than persons.

But man is not a thing. He must be dealt with not as an "animated tool" but as a person sacred in himself. To do otherwise is to depersonalize the potential person and desecrate what he is. So long as the Negro or any other member of a minority group is treated as a means to an end, the image of God is abused in him and consequently and proportionately lost by those who inflict the abuse.

Segregation is also morally wrong because it deprives man of freedom, that quality which makes him man. The very character of the life of man demands freedom. In speaking of freedom I am not referring to the freedom of a thing called the will. The very phrase, "freedom of the will," abstracts freedom from the person to make it an object; and an object almost by definition is not free. But freedom cannot thus be abstracted from the person, who is always subject as well as object and who himself still does the abstracting. So I am speaking of the freedom of man, the whole man, and not the freedom of a function called the will.

Neither am I implying that there are no limits to freedom. Freedom always operates within the limits of an already determined structure. Thus the mathematician is free to draw a circle, but he is not free to make a circle square. A man is free to walk through an open door, but he is not free to walk through a brick wall. A man is free to go to Chicago or New York, but he is not free to go to both cities at one and the same time. Freedom is always within destiny. It is the chosen fulfillment of our destined nature. We are always both free and destined.

The essence of man is found in freedom. This is what Paul Tillich means when he affirms, "Man is man because he is free," or what Tolstoy implies when he says, "I cannot conceive of a man not being free unless he is dead."

What is freedom? It is, first, the capacity to deliberate or to weigh alternatives. "Shall I be a doctor or a lawyer?" "Shall I be a Democrat, Republican or Socialist?" "Shall I be a humanist or a theist?" Moment by moment we go through life engaged in this strange conversation with ourselves. Second, freedom expresses itself in decision. The word "decision," like the word "incision," involves the image of cutting. Incision means to cut in, decision means to cut off. When I make a decision, I cut off alternatives and make a choice. The existentialists say we must choose, that we are choosing animals, and that if we do not choose, we sink into thinghood and the mass mind. A third expression of freedom is responsibility. This is the obligation of the person to respond if he is questioned about his decisions. No one else can respond for him. He alone must respond, for his acts are determined by the totality of his being.

The immorality of segregation is that it is a selfishly contrived system which cuts off one's capacity to deliberate, decide and respond.

The absence of freedom imposes restraint on my deliberations as to what I shall do, where I shall live or the kind of task I shall pursue. I am robbed of the basic quality of manness. When I cannot choose what I shall do or where I shall live, it means in fact that someone or some system has already made these decisions for me, and I am reduced to an animal. Then the only resemblance I have to a man is in my motor responses and functions. I cannot adequately assume responsibility as a person because I have been made the victim of a decision in which I played no part.

This is why segregation has wreaked havoc with the Negro. It is sometimes difficult to determine which are the deepest wounds, the physical or the psychological. Only a Negro understands the social leprosy that segregation inflicts upon him. Like a nagging ailment, it follows his every activity, leaving him tormented by day and haunted by night. The suppressed fears and resentments and the expressed anxieties and sensitivities make each day a life of turmoil. Every confrontation with the restrictions against him is another emotional battle in a never-ending war. Nothing can be more diabolical than a deliberate attempt to destroy in any man his will to be a man and to withhold from him that something which constitutes his true essence.

The church has an opportunity and a duty to lift up its voice like a trumpet and declare unto the people the immorality of segregation. It must affirm that every human life is a reflection of divinity, and that every act of injustice mars and defaces the image of God in man. The undergirding philosophy of segregation is diametrically opposed to the undergirding philosophy of our Judeo-Christian heritage, and all the dialectics of the logicians cannot make them lie down together.

But declarations against segregation, however sincere, are not enough. The church must take the lead in social reform. It must move out into the arena of life and do battle for the sanctity of religious commitments. And it must lead men along the path of true integration, something the law cannot do.

Genuine integration will come when men are obedient to the unenforceable. Dr. Harry Emerson Fosdick has made an impressive distinction between enforceable and unenforceable obligations. The former are regulated by the codes of society and the vigorous implementation of law-enforcement agencies. Breaking these obligations, spelled out on thousands of pages in lawbooks, has filled numberless prisons. But unenforceable obligations are beyond the reach of the laws of society. They concern inner attitudes, expressions of compassion which lawbooks cannot regulate and jails cannot rectify. Such obligations are met by one's commitment to an inner law, a law written on the heart. Man-made laws assure justice, but a higher law produces love. No code of conduct ever compelled a father to love his children or a husband to show affection to his wife. The law court may force him to provide bread for the family, but it cannot make him provide the bread of love. A good father is obedient to the unenforceable.

The ultimate solution to the race problem lies in the willingness of men to obey the unenforceable. Court orders and federal enforcement agencies are of inestimable value in achieving desegregation, but desegregation is only a partial, though necessary, step toward the final goal which we seek to realize, genuine intergroup and interpersonal living. Desegregation will break down the legal barriers and bring men together physically, but something must touch the hearts and souls of men so that they will come together spiritually because it is natural and right. A vigorous enforcement of civil rights will bring an end to segregated public facilities, but it cannot bring an end to fears, prejudice, pride and irrationality, which are the barriers to a truly integrated society. These dark and demonic responses will be removed only as men are possessed by the invisible inner law which etches on their hearts the conviction that all men are brothers and that love is mankind's most potent weapon for personal and social transformation. True integration will be achieved by men who are willingly obedient to unenforceable obligations.

In the final analysis the white man cannot ignore the Negro's problem, because he is a part of the Negro and the Negro is a part of him. The Negro's agony diminishes the white man, and the Negro's salvation enlarges the white man.

What is needed today on the part of white America is a committed altruism which recognizes this truth. True altruism is more than the capacity to pity; it is the capacity to empathize. Pity is feeling sorry for someone; empathy is feeling sorry with someone. Empathy is fellow feeling for the person in need—his pain, agony and burdens. I doubt if the problems of our teeming ghettos will have a great chance to be solved until the white majority, through genuine empathy, comes to feel the ache and anguish of the Negroes' daily life.

IV

The Dilemma of Negro Americans

The dilemma of white America is the source and cause of the dilemma of Negro America. Just as the ambivalence of white Americans grows out of their oppressor status, the predicament of Negro Americans grows out of their oppressed status. It is impossible for white Americans to grasp the depths and dimensions of the Negro's dilemma without understanding what it means to be a Negro in America. Of course it is not easy to perform this act of empathy. Putting oneself in another person's place is always fraught with difficulties. Over and over again it is said in the black ghettos of America that "no white person can ever understand what it means to be a Negro." There is good reason for this assumption, for there is very little in the life and experience of white America that can compare to the curse this society has put on color. And yet, if the present chasm of hostility, fear and distrust is to be bridged, the white man must begin to walk in the pathways of his black brothers and feel some of the pain and hurt that throb without letup in their daily lives.

The central quality in the Negro's life is pain—pain so old and so deep that it shows in almost every moment of his existence. It emerges in the cheerlessness of his sorrow songs, in the melancholy of his blues and in the pathos of his sermons. The Negro while laughing sheds invisible tears that no hand can wipe away. In a highly competitive world, the Negro knows that a cloud of persistent denial stands between him and the sun, between him and life and power, between him and whatever he needs. In the words of a noble black bard of yesteryear, Paul Laurence Dunbar:

> A crust of bread and a corner to sleep in,
> A minute to smile and an hour to weep in,
> A pint of joy to a peck of trouble,
> And never a laugh but the moans come double:
> And that is life![1]

Negro life! Being a Negro in America means being scarred by a history of slavery and family disorganization. Negroes have grown accustomed now to hearing unfeeling and insensitive whites say: "Other immigrant groups such as the Irish, the Jews and the Italians started out with similar handicaps, and yet they made it. Why haven't the Negroes done the same?" These questioners refuse to see that the situation of other immigrant groups a hundred years ago and the situation of the Negro today cannot be usefully compared. Negroes were brought here in chains long before the Irish decided *voluntarily* to leave Ireland or the Italians thought of leaving Italy. Some Jews may have left their homes in Europe involuntarily, but they were not in chains when they arrived on these shores. Other immigrant groups came to America with language and economic handicaps, but not with the stigma of color. Above all, no other ethnic group has been a slave on American soil, and no other group has had its family structure deliberately torn apart. This is the rub.

Today there is considerable discussion about the disintegration of the Negro family in the urban ghettos. We need only to learn something about the special origins of the Negro family to discover the root of the problem. The Negro family for three hundred years has been on the tracks of the racing locomotives of American history, dragged along mangled and crippled. Pettigrew has pointed out that American slavery is distinguished from all other forms of slavery because it consciously dehumanized the Negro. In Greece and Rome, for example, slaves preserved dignity and a measure of family life. Our institution of slavery, on the other hand, began with the breakup of families on the coasts of Africa. Because the middle passage was long and expensive, African families were torn apart in the interest of selectivity, as if the members were beasts. In the ships' holds, black captives were packed spoon fashion to live on a voyage often lasting two to six months in a space for each the size of a coffin. If water ran short, or famine threatened, or a plague broke out, whole cargoes of living and dead were thrown overboard. The sheer physical torture was sufficient to murder millions of men, women and children. But even more incalculable was the psychological damage.

Of those families who survived the voyage, many more were ripped apart on the auction block as soon as they reached American shores. Against this ghastly background the Negro family began life in the United States. On the plantation the institution of legal marriage for slaves did not exist. The masters might direct mating, or if they did not intervene, marriage occurred without sanctions. There were polygamous relationships, fragile monogamous relationships, illegitimacies, abandonment and the repetitive tearing apart of families as children, husbands or wives were sold to other plantations. But these cruel conditions were not yet the whole story. Masters and their sons used Negro women to satisfy their spontaneous lust or, when more humane attitudes prevailed, as concubines. The depths were reached in Virginia, which we sentimentally call the State of Presidents. There slaves were bred for sale, not casually or incidentally, but in a vast deliberate program which produced enormous wealth for slaveowners. This breeding program was one answer to the legal halting of the slave traffic early in the nineteenth century.

Against these odds the Negro family struggled to survive through the antebellum era, and miraculously many did. In all this psychological and physical horror many slaves managed to hold on to their children and developed warmth and affection and family loyalties against the smashing tides of emotional corruption and destruction.

The liberation from slavery in 1863, which should have initiated the birth of a stable Negro family life, meant a formal legal freedom but, as Henrietta Buckmaster put it, "With Appomattox, four million black people in the South owned their skins and nothing more." With civil war still dividing the nation, a new inferno engulfed the Negro and his family. Thrown off the plantations, penniless, homeless, still largely in the territory of their enemies and in the grip of fear, bewilderment and aimlessness, hundreds of thousands became wanderers. For security they fled to Union Army camps that were unprepared to help. One writer describes a mother carrying a child in one arm, a father holding another child, and eight other children with their hands tied to one rope held by the mother, who struggled after Sherman's army and traveled hundreds of miles to safety. All were not so fortunate. In the starvation-induced madness some Negroes killed their children to free them of their misery.

These are historical facts. If they cause the mind to reel with horror, it is still necessary to realize that this is but a tiny glimpse of the reality of the era, and it does justice neither to the enormous extent of the tragedy nor to the degree of human suffering and sorrow.

Following the Civil War, millions returned to a new form of slavery, once again imprisoned on plantations devoid of human rights and plunged into searing poverty generation after generation. Some families found their way to the North, in a movement E. Franklin Frazier aptly describes as "into the city of destruction." Illiterate, afraid and crushed by want, they were herded into the slums. The bewildering complexity of the city undermined the confidence of fathers and mothers, causing them to lose control of their children, whose bewilderment was even more acute.

Once more the Negro's problem had two cutting edges. Because the institution of marriage had been illegal under slavery, and because of indiscriminate sex relations, often with their white masters, mothers could identify their children but frequently not their children's fathers. Moreover, the women, being more generally in the house and charged with the care of the white master's children, were more often exposed to some education and a sense—though minimal—of personal worth. Hence a matriarchy had early developed. After slavery it persisted because in the cities there was more employment for women than for men. Though both were unskilled, the women could be used in domestic service at low wages. The woman became the support of the household and the matriarchy was reinforced. The Negro male existed in a larger society dominated by men, but he was subordinated to women in his own society.

The quest of the Negro male for employment was always frustrating. If he lacked skill, he was only occasionally wanted because such employment as he could find had little regularity and even less remuneration. If he had a skill, he also had his black skin, and discrimination locked doors against him. In the competition for scarce jobs he was a loser because he was born that way.

His rage and torment were frequently turned inward, because if they gained outward expression their consequences could be fatal. The Negro father became resigned to hopelessness, and he communicated this to his children. Some men, unable to contain the emotional storms, struck out at those who would be least likely to destroy them. They beat their wives and their children in order to protest a social injustice, and the tragedy was that none of them understood why the violence exploded.

The shattering blows on the Negro family have made it fragile, deprived and often psychopathic. This is doubly tragic because nothing is so much needed as a secure family life for a people seeking to rise out of poverty and backwardness. History continues to mock the Negro today, because just as he needs ever greater family integrity, severe strains are assailing family life in the white community. Delinquency is not confined to the underprivileged; it is rampant among the middle and upper social strata, and more than one observer argues that juvenile delinquency is a product of widespread adult delinquency. In short, the larger society is not at this time a constructive educational force for the Negro.

The dark side of the picture appears to make the future bleak, if not hopeless. Yet something says this is not true. Back on the coasts of Africa, mothers fought slave traders fiercely to save their children. They offered their bodies to slavers if they would leave the children behind. On some slave ships that are known, and many that will never be known, manacled Negroes crawled from the holds and fought unarmed against guns and knives. On slave plantations parents fought, stole, sacrificed and died for their families. After liberation countless mothers wandered over roadless states looking for the children who had been taken from them and sold. And finally, in the past decade mothers, fathers and their children have marched together against clubs, guns, cattle prods and mobs, not for conquest but only to be allowed to live as humans. The Negro was crushed, battered and brutalized, but he never gave up. He proves again that life is stronger than death. The Negro family is scarred; it is submerged; but it struggles to survive.

A hundred times I have been asked why we have allowed little children to march in demonstrations, to freeze and suffer in jails, to be exposed to bullets and dynamite. The questions imply that we have revealed a want of family feeling or a recklessness toward family security. The answer is simple. Our children and our families are maimed a little every day of our lives. If we can end an incessant torture by a single climactic confrontation, the risks are acceptable. Moreover, our family life will be born anew if we fight together. Other families may be fortunate enough to be able to protect their young from danger. Our families, as we have seen, are different. Oppression has again and again divided and splintered them. We are a people torn apart from era to era. It is logical, moral and psychologically constructive for us to resist oppression united as families. Out of this unity, out of the bond of fighting together, forges will come. The inner strength and integrity will make us whole again.

The most optimistic element revealed in any review of the Negro family's experience is that the causes for its present crisis are culturally and socially induced. What man has torn down, he can rebuild. At the root of the difficulty in Negro life today is pervasive and persistent economic want. To grow from within, the Negro family—and especially the Negro man—needs only fair opportunity for jobs, education, housing and access to culture. To be strengthened from the outside requires protection from the grim exploitation that has haunted the Negro for three hundred years.

The Negro family lived in nature's jungle in Africa and subdued the hostile environment. In the United States it has lived in a man-made social and psychological jungle which it could not subdue. Many have been destroyed by it. Yet others have survived and developed a formidable capacity for hardships. It is on this strength that society must now begin to build.

As public awareness of the predicament of the Negro family increases, there will be danger and opportunity. The opportunity will be to deal fully rather than haphazardly with the problem as a whole—to see it as a social catastrophe brought on by long years of brutality and oppression and to meet it as other disasters are met, with an adequacy of resources. The danger will be that the problems will be attributed to innate Negro weaknesses and used to justify further neglect and to rationalize continued oppression.

Many of the ugly pages of American history have been obscured and forgotten. A society is always eager to cover misdeeds with a cloak of forgetfulness, but no society can fully repress an ugly past when the ravages persist into the present. America owes a debt of justice which it has only begun to pay. If it loses the will to finish or slackens in its determination, history will recall its crimes and the country that would be great will lack the most indispensable element of greatness—justice.

Being a Negro in America means not only living with the consequences of a past of slavery and family disorganization, but facing this very day the pangs of "color shock." Because the society, with unmitigated cruelty, has made the Negro's color anathema, every Negro child suffers a traumatic emotional burden when he encounters the reality of his black skin. In Dr. Kenneth Clark's classic study, *Prejudice and Your Child*,[2] there is a simple test for color sensitivity in young children. This involves having a child draw a tree, an apple and a child, and then proceed to color each one at will. One of my colleagues reports conducting this test with his three-year-old daughter. The child, holding the crayon deftly and delicately, colored the tree green and then in the same way shaded the apple red. But when it came to coloring the child, she gripped the crayon with her fist and in a violent pattern of chaotic motions made purple slashes across the figure.

This was a child living in a Long Island suburb, not in the Deep South. Her parents were well educated and sensitive to the child's emotional health, but in America there is no escape from the awareness of color and the fact that our society places a qualitative difference on a person of dark skin.

Every Negro comes face to face with this color shock, and it constitutes a major emotional crisis. It is accompanied by a sort of fatiguing, wearisome hopelessness. If one is rejected because he is uneducated, he can at least be consoled by the fact that it may be possible for him to get an education. If one is rejected because he is low on the economic ladder, he can at least dream of the day that he will rise from his dungeon of economic deprivation. If one is rejected because he speaks with an accent, he can at least, if he desires, work to bring his speech in line with the dominant group. If, however, one is rejected because of his color, he must face the anguishing fact that he is being rejected because of something in himself that cannot be changed. All prejudice is evil, but the prejudice that rejects a man because of the color of his skin is the most despicable expression of man's inhumanity to man.

Being a Negro in America means being herded in ghettos, or reservations, being constantly ignored and made to feel invisible. You long to be seen, to be heard, to be respected. But it is like blowing in the wind. As I think about the anatomy of the ghetto, I am often reminded of a passage from W. E. B. Du Bois's autobiography, *Dusk of Dawn:*

> It is difficult to let others see the full psychological meaning of caste segregation. It is as though one, looking out from a dark cave in a side of an impending mountain, sees the world passing and speaks to it; speaks courteously and persuasively, showing them how these entombed souls are hindered in their natural movement, expression, and development; and how their loosening from prison would be a matter not simply of courtesy, sympathy, and help to them, but aid to all the world. One talks on evenly and logically in this way but notices that the passing throng does not even turn its head, or if it does, glances curiously and walks on. It gradually penetrates the minds of the prisoners that the people passing do not hear; that some thick sheet of invisible but horribly tangible plate glass is between them and the world. . . . Then the people within may become hysterical. They may scream and hurl themselves against the barriers, hardly realizing in their bewilderment that they are screaming in a vacuum unheard and that their antics may actually seem funny to those outside looking in. They may even, here and there, break through in blood and disfigurement, and find themselves faced by a horrified, implacable, and quite overwhelming mob of people frightened for their own very existence.[3]

Most people are totally unaware of the darkness of the cave in which the Negro is forced to live. A few individuals can break out, but the vast majority remain its prisoners. Our cities have constructed elaborate expressways and elevated skyways, and white Americans speed from suburb to inner city through vast pockets of black deprivation without ever getting a glimpse of the suffering and misery in their midst.

But while so many white Americans are unaware of conditions inside the ghetto, there are very few ghetto dwellers who are unaware of the life outside. Their television sets bombard them day by day with the opulence of the larger society. From behind the ghetto walls they see glistening towers of glass and steel springing up almost overnight. They hear jet liners speeding over their heads at six hundred miles an hour. They hear of satellites streaking through outer space and revealing details of the moon.

Then they begin to think of their own conditions. They know that they are always given the hardest, ugliest, most menial work to do. They look at these impressive buildings under construction and realize that almost certainly they cannot get those well-paying construction jobs, because building trade unions reserve them for whites only. They know that people who built the bridges, the mansions and docks of the South could build modern buildings if they were only given a chance for apprenticeship training. They realize that it is hard, raw discrimination that shuts them out. It is not only poverty that torments the Negro; it is the fact of poverty amid plenty. It is a misery generated by the gulf between the affluence he sees in the mass media and the deprivation he experiences in his everyday life.

Living with the daily ugliness of slum life, educational castration and economic exploitation, some ghetto dwellers now and then strike out in spasms of violence and self-defeating riots. A riot is at bottom the language of the unheard. It is the desperate, suicidal cry of one who is so fed up with the powerlessness of his cave existence that he asserts that he would rather be dead than ignored.

Touring Watts a few days after that nightmarish riot in 1965, Bayard Rustin, Andrew Young and I confronted a group of youngsters who said to us joyously, "We won."

We asked them: "How can you say you won when thirty-four Negroes are dead, your community is destroyed, and whites are using the riot as an excuse for inaction?"

Their answer: "We won because we made them pay attention to us."

As long as people are ignored, as long as they are voiceless, as long as they are trampled by the iron feet of exploitation, there is the danger that they, like little children, will have their emotional outbursts which will break out in violence in the streets.

The amazing thing about the ghetto is that so few Negroes have rioted. Ninety-nine percent of American Negroes have never thrown a Molotov cocktail or lit a match to comply with the admonition, "Burn, baby, burn." Even more amazing is the fact that so many ghetto inhabitants have maintained hope in the midst of hopeless conditions. Contrary to the myth held by many white Americans, the ghetto is not a monolithic unit of dope addicts, alcoholics, prostitutes and unwed mothers. There are churches in the ghetto as well as bars. There are stable families in the ghetto as well as illegitimacies. Ninety percent of the young people of the ghetto never come in conflict with the law. We are constantly made aware of desertions and illegitimacies that take place in the ghetto, but often forget the vast majority of families that have stayed together throughout the years. Despite the overwhelming odds, the majority of Negroes in the ghetto go on living, go on striving, go on hoping. This is the miracle. To be a Negro in America is often to hope against hope. It means fighting daily a double battle—a battle against pathology within and a battle against oppression without.

For the past year I have been living and working in the ghettos of Chicago. There the problems of poverty and despair are graphically illustrated. The phone rings daily with countless stories of man's inhumanity to man, and I find myself struggling constantly against the depression and hopelessness which the hearts of our cities pump into the spiritual bloodstream of our lives.

This is truly an island of poverty in the midst of an ocean of plenty, for Chicago now boasts the highest per capita income of any city in the world. But you would never believe it looking out of the windows of my apartment in the slum of Lawndale. From this vantage point you see only hundreds of children playing in the streets, and when you go out and talk to them you see the light of intelligence glowing in their beautiful dark eyes. Then you realize their overwhelming joy because someone has simply stopped to say hello; for they live in a world where even their parents are often forced to ignore them. In the tight squeeze of economic pressure, their mothers and fathers both must work; indeed, more often than not, the father will hold two jobs, one in the day and another at night. With the long distances ghetto parents must travel to work and the emotional exhaustion that comes from the daily struggle to survive in a hostile world, they are left with too little time or energy to attend to the emotional needs of their growing children.

Too soon you begin to see the effects of this emotional and environmental deprivation. The children's clothes are too skimpy to protect them from the Chicago wind, and a closer look reveals the mucus in the corners of their bright eyes, and you are reminded that vitamin pills and flu shots are luxuries which they can ill afford. The "runny noses" of ghetto children become a graphic symbol of medical neglect in a society which has mastered most of the diseases from which they will too soon die. There is something wrong in a society which allows this to happen.

Last summer our own children lived with us in Lawndale, and it was only a few days before we became aware of the change in their behavior. Their tempers flared and they sometimes reverted to almost infantile behavior. As riots raged around them outside, I realized that the crowded flat in which we lived was about to produce an emotional explosion in my own family. It was just too hot, too crowded, too devoid of creative forms of recreation. There was just not space enough in the neighborhood to run off the energy of childhood without running into busy, traffic-laden streets. And I understood anew the conditions which make of the ghetto an emotional pressure cooker.

One can only assume that the determining factor in the destiny of the children of Lawndale and other ghettos is their color. The evidence of the schools is persuasive. Statistics revealed in 1964 that Chicago spent an average of $366 a year per pupil in predominantly white schools and from $450 to $900 a year per pupil for suburban white neighborhoods, but the Negro neighborhoods received only $266 per year per pupil. In this way the system conspires to perpetuate inferior status and to prepare the Negro for those tasks that no one else wants, hence creating a mass of unskilled, cheap labor for the society at large. Already in childhood their lives are crushed mentally, emotionally and physically, and then society develops the myth of inferiority to give credence to its lifelong patterns of exploitation, which can only be defined as our system of slavery in the twentieth century.

As adults, my neighbors pay more rent in the substandard slums of Lawndale than the whites must pay for modern apartments in the suburbs. The median rent in Lawndale is $90 per month for four and a half rooms without utilities, usually without heat on a regular basis, and with only the most spasmodic janitorial services. Whites in the suburbs of Gage Park, South Deering and Belmont-Cragen pay a median rent of less than $80 per month for five and a half rooms.

The situation is much the same for consumer goods, purchase prices on homes and a variety of other services. Consumer items range from five to twelve cents higher in the ghetto stores than in the suburban stores, both run by the same supermarket chains; and numerous stores in the ghetto have been the subject of community protests against the sale of spoiled meats and vegetables. This exploitation is possible because so many of the residents of the ghetto have no personal means of transportation. It is a vicious circle. You can't get a job because you are poorly educated, and you must depend on welfare to feed your children; but if you receive public aid in Chicago, you cannot own property, not even an automobile, so you are condemned to the jobs and shops which are closest to your home. Once confined to this isolated community, one no longer participates in a free economy, but is subject to price-fixing and wholesale robbery by many of the merchants of the area.

The Chicago Urban League has documented a 10–20 percent "color tax" which applies on virtually every product purchased in the segregated community. This is especially true of housing, for the color tax is applied in every step of the transaction. First, it swells the purchase price of the house, for the demand for homes by Negroes far exceeds the supply, and as long as theirs are closed communities, Negroes will be forced to pay more. Next it is applied by the banking and lending institutions, who declare the Negro a poor credit risk and charge him exorbitant interest rates or refuse him traditional loans and thereby force him to buy homes on "contract."

Finally, when a man is able to make his way through the maze of handicaps and get just one foot out of the jungle of poverty and exploitation, he is subject to the whims of the political and economic giants of the city, which move in impersonally to crush the little flower of success that has just begun to bloom.

One illustration is the community of Englewood in Chicago. Englewood is 85 percent Negro. It is made up of people who have worked and saved to become homeowners. One such homeowner is a redcap in the railroad station who was somehow able to purchase a home for $17,000. Now the Urban Renewal Authority has claimed his home along with six hundred others, not because they are deteriorating or substandard but because the shopping center wants additional parking space. The house was appraised at the normal market price of $14,000, rather than the inflated Negro market price of $17,000, after only four years' occupancy, during which time all real estate values in the Chicago area were on the increase.

These families have appealed to the local and national offices of Urban Renewal, and even taken their case into federal court, but to no avail. The city continues to acquire land and evict families, returning them to the slums from whence they came, deeper in debt, bitter and resentful, with no voice or hope of redress. All attempts to offer alternative proposals, such as double-decking the present parking areas, have been ignored.

Here the democratic process breaks down, for the rights of the individual voter are impossible to organize without adequate funds, while the business community supplies the existing political machine with enough funds to organize massive campaigns and control mass media.

Here, too, the North reveals its true ambivalence on the subject of civil rights. When, in the last session of Congress, the issue came home to the North through a call for open housing legislation, white Northern congressmen who had enthusiastically supported the 1964 and 1965 civil rights bills now joined in a mighty chorus of anguish and dismay reminiscent of Alabama and Mississippi. So the first piece of legislation aimed at rectifying a shocking evil in the North went down to crushing defeat.

Nothing today more clearly indicates the residue of racism still lodging in our society than the responses of white America to integrated housing. Here the tides of prejudice, fear and irrationality rise to flood proportions. This is not a new backlash caused by the Black Power movement; there had been no ominous riots in Watts when white Californians defeated a fair housing bill in 1964. The present resistance to open housing is based on the same premises that came into being to rationalize slavery. It is rooted in the fear that the alleged depravity or defective nature of the out-race will infiltrate the neighborhood of the in-race.

The potential presence of a Negro in a previously all-white neighborhood often arouses hostility and causes panic selling. The question of the character of the potential Negro neighbor is not a matter of inquiry. If it were, a Cicero, Illinois, would welcome a Ralph Bunche into the community rather than an Al Capone. The fact that professional white hoodlums and racketeers are located in the best neighborhoods of Cicero is fit proof that the opposition to open housing is not based on behavior or moral standards. The reason Ralph Bunche could not live in Cicero is that he is a Negro, pure and simple. His individual culture, brilliance and character are not considered. To the racist, he, like every Negro, lacks individuality. He is part of a defective group.

Just as the doctrine of white supremacy came into being to justify the profitable system of slavery, through shrewd and subtle ways some realtors perpetrate the same racist doctrine to justify the profitable real estate business. Real estate brokers build up financial empires by keeping the housing market closed. Going into white neighborhoods where a few Negroes have moved in, they urge the whites to leave because their property values will depreciate. Thereupon, the real estate broker makes a huge profit from the whites that must be relocated and a doubly huge profit from the Negroes, who, in desperate search for better housing, often pay twice as much for a house as it is worth.

Many whites who oppose open housing would deny that they are racists. They turn to sociological arguments—the crime rate in the Negro community, the lagging cultural standards, the fear that their schools will become academically inferior, the fear that property values will depreciate —in order to find excuses for their opposition. They never stop to realize that criminal responses are environmental, not racial. To hem a people up in the prison walls of overcrowded ghettos and to confine them in rat-infested slums is to breed crime, whatever the racial group may be. It is a strange and twisted logic to use the tragic results of segregation as an argument for its continuation. As to the argument that Negroes depreciate property values, study after study has revealed that it is usually the other way around. When Negroes move into a neighborhood and whites refuse to flee, property values are more likely to increase. It is only when blockbusting takes place and whites begin to move out that property values decrease.

However much it is denied, however many excuses are

made, the hard cold fact is that many white Americans oppose open housing because they unconsciously, and often
consciously, feel that the Negro is innately inferior, impure,
depraved and degenerate. It is a contemporary expression of
America's long dalliance with racism and white supremacy.

No Negro escapes this cycle of modern slavery. Even the
new Negro middle class often finds itself in ghettoized housing and in jobs at the mercy of the white world. Some of the
most tragic figures in our society now are the Negro company vice presidents who sit with no authority or influence
because they were merely employed for window dressing in
an effort to win the Negro market or to comply with federal
regulations in Title VII of the 1964 Civil Rights Act.

And so being a Negro in America is not a comfortable existence. It means being a part of the company of the bruised,
the battered, the scarred and the defeated. Being a Negro
in America means trying to smile when you want to cry. It
means trying to hold on to physical life amid psychological
death. It means the pain of watching your children grow up
with clouds of inferiority in their mental skies. It means having your legs cut off, and then being condemned for being
a cripple. It means seeing your mother and father spiritually murdered by the slings and arrows of daily exploitation,
and then being hated for being an orphan. Being a Negro
in America means listening to suburban politicians talk el-
oquently against open housing while arguing in the same
breath that they are not racists. It means being harried by day
and haunted by night by a nagging sense of nobodyness and
constantly fighting to be saved from the poison of bitterness.
It means the ache and anguish of living in so many situations
where hopes unborn have died.

After 348 years racial injustice is still the Negro's burden
and America's shame. Yet for his own inner health and outer

functioning, the Negro is called upon to be as resourceful, as productive and as responsible as those who have not known such oppression and exploitation. *This is the Negro's dilemma.* He who starts behind in a race must forever remain behind or run faster than the man in front. What a dilemma! It is a call to do the impossible. It is enough to cause the Negro to give up in despair.

And yet there are times when life demands the perpetual doing of the impossible. The life of our slave forebears is eternal testimony to the ability of men to achieve the impossible. So, too, we must embark upon this difficult, trying and sometimes bewildering course. With a dynamic will, we must transform our minus into a plus, and move on aggressively through the storms of injustice and the jostling winds of daily handicaps, toward the beaconing lights of fulfillment. Our dilemma is serious and our handicaps are real. But equally real is the power of a creative will and its ability to give us the courage to go on "in spite of."

Once when Ole Bull, the Norwegian violinist, was giving a concert in Paris, his A string snapped. Instead of stopping, Ole Bull transposed the composition and finished the concert on three strings. This is what the Negro confronts. Through years of unjust oppression and unmerited suffering our A strings of opportunity have snapped. But the performance of our lives must go on, and without self-pity or surrender we must go forward on three strings. Our lives will be comparable to the Battle of Marengo—in the morning an obvious defeat, in the afternoon a resounding victory. It is something of what Langston Hughes expresses in his poem "Mother to Son":

Well, son, I'll tell you:
Life for me ain't been no crystal stair.

It's had tacks in it,
And splinters,
And boards torn up,
And places with no carpet on the floor—
Bare.
But all the time
I'se been a-climbin' on,
And reachin' landin's,
And turnin' corners,
And sometimes goin' in the dark
Where there ain't been no light.
So, boy, don't you turn back.
Don't you set down on the steps
'Cause you finds it kinder hard,
Don't you fall now—
For I'se still goin,' honey,
I'se still climbin,'
And life for me ain't been no crystal stair.[4]

This is the challenge facing every Negro. It is this determination to "keep climbing" that will transform the dark into light.

II

What, then, are the challenges that the Negro faces as a result of his dilemma?

There is always the understandable temptation to seek negative and self-destructive solutions. Some seek a passive way out by yielding to the feeling of inferiority; or by allowing the floodgates of defeat to open with an avalanche of despair; or by dropping out of school; or by turning to the escape valves of narcotics and alcohol. Others seek a defiant way out. Through antisocial behavior, overt delinquency and gang warfare, they release their pent-up vindictiveness on the whole society. Meanness becomes their dominating characteristic. They trust no one and do not expect others to trust them. Still others seek to deal with the dilemma through the path of isolation. They have the fantasy of a separate black state or a separate black nation within the nation. This approach is the most cynical and nihilistic of all, because it is based on a loss of faith in the possibilities of American democracy.

The shattered dreams and blasted hopes of the Negro's daily life provide the psychological and sociological explanation for the choice by some of negative paths of escape. A society that has treated a whole race of people as flotsam and jetsam in the river of life cannot expect all of them to grow up healthy and well balanced. But in spite of these explanations the Negro cannot constructively deal with his dilemma through negative strategies. In spite of uncertainties and vicissitudes we must develop the courage to confront the negatives of circumstance with the positives of inner determination.

One positive response to our dilemma is to develop a rugged sense of somebodyness. The tragedy of slavery and segregation is that they instilled in the Negro a disastrous sense of his own worthlessness. To overcome this terrible feeling of being less than human, the Negro must assert for all to hear and see a majestic sense of his worth. There is such a thing as a desegregated mind. We must no longer allow the outer chains of an oppressive society to shackle our minds. With courage and fearlessness we must set out daringly to stabilize our egos. This alone will give us a confirmation of our roots and a validation of our worth.

This sense of somebodyness means the refusal to be ashamed of being black. Our children must be taught to stand tall with their heads proudly lifted. We need not be duped into purchasing bleaching creams that promise to make us lighter. We need not process our hair to make it appear straight. Whether some men, black and white, realize it or not, black people are very beautiful. Life's piano can only produce the melodies of brotherhood when it is recognized that the black keys are as basic, necessary and beautiful as the white keys. The Negro, through self-acceptance and self-appreciation, will one day cause white America to see that integration is not an obstacle, but an opportunity to participate in the beauty of diversity.

Courage, the determination not to be overwhelmed by any object, that power of the mind capable of sloughing off the thingification of the past, will be the Negro's most potent weapon in achieving self-respect. Something of the inner spirit of our slave forebears must be pursued today. From the inner depths of our being we must sing with them: "Before I'll be a slave, I'll be buried in my grave and go home to my Lord and be free." This spirit, this drive, this rugged sense of somebodyness is the first and most vital step that the Negro must take in dealing with his dilemma.

A second important step that the Negro must take is to work passionately for group identity. This does not mean group isolation or group exclusivity. It means the kind of group consciousness that Negroes need in order to participate more meaningfully at all levels of the life of our nation.

Group unity necessarily involves group trust and reconciliation. One of the most serious effects of the Negro's damaged ego has been his frequent loss of respect for himself and for other Negroes. He ends up with an ambivalence toward his own kind. To overcome this tragic conflict, it will be necessary for the Negro to find a new self-image. Only by being reconciled to ourselves will we be able to build upon the resources we already have at our disposal. Too many Negroes are jealous of other Negroes' successes and progress. Too many Negro organizations are warring against each other with a claim to absolute truth. The Pharaohs had a favorite and effective strategy to keep their slaves in bondage: keep them fighting among themselves. The divide-and-conquer technique has been a potent weapon in the arsenal of oppression. But when slaves unite, the Red Seas of history open and the Egypts of slavery crumble.

This plea for unity is not a call for uniformity. There must always be healthy debate. There will be inevitable differences of opinion. The dilemma that the Negro confronts is so complex and monumental that its solution will of necessity involve a diversified approach. But Negroes can differ and still unite around common goals.

There are already structured forces in the Negro community that can serve as the basis for building a powerful united front—the Negro church, the Negro press, the Negro fraternities and sororities, and Negro professional associations. We must admit that these forces have never given their full resources to the cause of Negro liberation. There are still too many Negro churches that are so absorbed in a future good "over yonder" that they condition their members to adjust to the present evils "over here." Too many Negro newspapers have veered away from their traditional role as protest organs agitating for social change, and have turned to the sensational and the conservative in place of the substantive and the militant. Too many Negro social and professional groups have degenerated into snobbishness and a preoccupation with frivolities and trivial activity. But the failures of the past must not be an excuse for the inaction of the present and the future. These groups must be mobilized and motivated. This form of group unity can do infinitely more to liberate the Negro than any action of *individuals*. We have been oppressed as a group and we must overcome that oppression as a group.

Through this form of group unity we can begin a constructive program which will vigorously seek to improve our personal standards. It is not a sign of weakness, but a sign of high maturity, to rise to the level of self-criticism. Through group unity we must convey to one another that our women must be respected, and that life is too precious to be destroyed in a Saturday night brawl, or a gang execution. Through community agencies and religious institutions we must develop a positive program through which Negro youth can become adjusted to urban living and improve their general level of behavior. While I strongly disagree with their separatist black supremacy philosophy, I have nothing but admiration for what our Muslim brothers have done to rehabilitate ex-convicts, dope addicts and men and women who, through despair and self-hatred, have sunk to moral degeneracy. This must be attempted on a much larger scale, and without the negative overtones that accompany Black Muslimism.

Since crime often grows out of a sense of futility and hopelessness, Negro parents, in spite of almost insuperable economic obstacles, must be urged to give their children the love, attention and sense of belonging that an oppressive society deprives them of. While not ignoring the fact that the ultimate way to diminish our problems of crime, family disorganization, illegitimacy and so forth will have to be found through a government program to help the frustrated Negro male find his true masculinity by placing him on his own two economic feet, we must do all within our power to approach these goals ourselves.

There is a third thing that the Negro must do to grapple

with his dilemma. We must make full and constructive use of the freedom we already possess. We must not wait until the day of full emancipation before we set out to make our individual and collective contributions to the life of our nation. Even though slavery and segregation were designed to make the Negro adjust patiently to mediocrity, we must work assiduously to aspire to excellence. This is particularly relevant for the young Negro. Realism impels us to admit that many older Negroes have been so scarred by long years of oppression, by limited or no education, that they can no longer be expected to achieve excellence. There are also some Negro youth who have faced so many closed doors and so many crippling defeats that they have lost motivation. For those youth who are alienated from the routines of work, there should be subsidized work situations which permit flexibility so that they can be carried along until they can manage the demands of the typical work place.

But there are a host of Negro youth who still have the will and the capacity to achieve excellence in their various fields of endeavor. Doors of opportunity are gradually opening now that were not open to our mothers and fathers. The great challenge is to prepare ourselves to enter these doors as they open.

We already have the inspiring examples of Negroes who with determination have broken through the shackles of circumstance. From an old slave cabin in Virginia's hills, Booker T. Washington rose to become one of America's great leaders. From the oppressive hills of Gordon County, Georgia, and the arms of a mother who could neither read nor write, Roland Hayes emerged as a singer whose melodious voice was heard in the palaces of kings and the mansions of queens. Coming from a poverty-stricken environment in Philadelphia, Pennsylvania, Marian Anderson became a distinguished contralto so honored by the world that Toscanini said a voice like hers comes only once in a century, and Sibelius exclaimed that his roof was too low for such a voice. From crippling beginnings, George Washington Carver created for himself an imperishable niche in the annals of science. From the racist bastion of Laurel, Mississippi, Leontyne Price, with a majestic soprano and a brilliant dramatic talent, rose to the heights of the Metropolitan Opera. Ralph J. Bunche, the grandson of a slave preacher, sits near the top in the ranks of world government.

There was a star in the poetic sky, and then came James Weldon Johnson, Paul Laurence Dunbar, Countee Cullen, Claude McKay and Langston Hughes to reach up and touch it. As musical artists and performers, Harry Belafonte singing the folk songs of every culture, Sammy Davis exclaiming "Yes I Can," Mahalia Jackson belting out the powerful gospel songs of the Negro church, Ray Charles sighing the blues, Duke Ellington pouring forth his superb jazz and Sidney Poitier acting with powerful talent have all reached the zenith of achievement and fame. The eloquent pens of Negro writers like W. E. B. Du Bois, Richard Wright, Ralph Ellison and James Baldwin have left their literary marks on the sands of time. From years of exclusion and denial Joe Louis, Jack Johnson, Muhammad Ali, Jackie Robinson, Roy Campanella, Don Newcombe, Willie Mays, Henry Aaron, Frank Robinson, James Brown, Bill Russell, Wilt Chamberlain, Jesse Owens, Buddy Young, Althea Gibson and Arthur Ashe all rose to the heights of the athletic world. These are only a few of the examples which remind us that, in spite of our lack of full freedom, we can make a contribution here and now.

Not all men are called to specialized or professional jobs; even fewer rise to the heights of genius; many are called to be laborers in the factories, fields and streets. But no work is insignificant. All labor that uplifts humanity has dignity and worth and should be pursued with respect for excellence. This clear onward drive to make full and creative use of the opportunities already available to us will be of immeasurable value in helping us to deal constructively with our agonizing dilemma.

The fourth challenge we face is to unite around powerful action programs to eradicate the last vestiges of racial injustice. We will be greatly misled if we feel that the problem will work itself out. Structures of evil do not crumble by passive waiting. If history teaches anything, it is that evil is recalcitrant and determined, and never voluntarily relinquishes its hold short of an almost fanatical resistance. Evil must be attacked by a counteracting persistence, by the day-to-day assault of the battering rams of justice.

We must get rid of the false notion that there is some miraculous quality in the flow of time that inevitably heals all evils. There is only one thing certain about time, and that is that it waits for no one. If it is not used constructively, it passes you by.

In this generation the children of darkness are still shrewder than the children of light. They are always zealous and conscientious in using time for their evil purposes. If they want to preserve segregation and tyranny, they do not wait on time; they make time their fellow conspirator. If they want to defeat a fair housing bill, they don't say to the public, "Be patient, wait on time, and our cause will win." Rather, they use time to spend big money, to disseminate half-truths, to confuse the popular mind. But the forces of light cautiously wait, patiently pray and timidly act. So we end up with a double destruction: the destructive violence of the bad people and the destructive silence of the good people.

Equally fallacious is the notion that ethical appeals and persuasion alone will bring about justice. This does not mean that ethical appeals must not be made. It simply means that those appeals must be undergirded by some form of constructive coercive power. If the Negro does not add persistent pressure to his patient plea, he will end up empty-handed. In a not too distant yesterday, Booker T. Washington tried this path of patient persuasion. I do not share the notion that he was an Uncle Tom who compromised for the sake of keeping the peace. Washington sincerely believed that if the South was not pushed too hard, that if the South was not forced to do something that it did not for the moment want to do, it would voluntarily rally in the end to the Negro's cause. Washington's error was that he underestimated the structures of evil; as a consequence his philosophy of pressureless persuasion only served as a springboard for racist Southerners to dive into deeper and more ruthless oppression of the Negro.

So every ethical appeal to the conscience of the white man must be accomplished by nonviolent pressure. If first-class citizenship is to become a reality for the Negro, he must through a powerful action program assume the primary responsibility for making it so.

The only answer to the delay, double-dealing, tokenism and racism that we still confront is through mass nonviolent action and the ballot. At times these may seem too slow and inadequate, but they are the only real tools we have. Our course of action must lie neither in passively relying on persuasion nor in actively succumbing to violent rebellion, but in a higher synthesis that reconciles the truths of these two opposites while avoiding the inadequacies and ineffectiveness of both. With the person relying on persuasion, we must agree that we will not violently destroy life or property; but we must balance this by agreeing with the person of violence that evil must be resisted. By so doing we avoid the nonresistance of the former and the violent resistance of the latter. With nonviolent resistance, we need not submit to any wrong, nor need we resort to violence in order to right a wrong.

The American racial revolution has been a revolution to "get in" rather than to overthrow. We want a share in the American economy, the housing market, the educational system and the social opportunities. This goal itself indicates that a social change in America must be nonviolent. If one is in search of a better job, it does not help to burn down the factory. If one needs more adequate education, shooting the principal will not help. If housing is the goal, only building and construction will produce that end. To destroy anything, person or property, cannot bring us closer to the goal that we seek.

So far, we have had constitutional backing for most of our demands for change, and this has made our work easier, since we could be sure of legal support from the federal courts. Now we are approaching areas where the voice of the Constitution is not clear. We have left the realm of constitutional rights and we are entering the area of human rights.

The Constitution assured the right to vote, but there is no such assurance of the right to adequate housing, or the right to an adequate income. And yet, in a nation which has a gross national product of $750 billion a year, it is morally right to insist that every person have a decent house, an adequate education and enough money to provide basic necessities for one's family. Achievement of these goals will be a lot more difficult and require much more discipline, understanding, organization and sacrifice.

Mass nonviolent action will continue to be one of the most effective tactics of the freedom movement. Many, especially in the North, argue that the maximum use of legislation, welfare and antipoverty programs has now replaced demonstrations, and that overt and visible protest should now be abandoned. Nothing could prove more erroneous than to demobilize at this point. It was the mass-action movement that engendered the changes of the decade, but the needs which created it are not yet satisfied. Without the will to unity and struggle Negroes would have no strength, and reversal of our successes could be easily effected. The use of creative tensions that broke the barriers of the South will be as indispensable in the North to obtain and extend necessary objectives.

But mass nonviolent demonstrations will not be enough. They must be supplemented by a continuing job of organization. To produce change, people must be organized to work together in units of power. These units may be political, as in the case of voters' leagues and political parties; they may be economic, as in the case of groups of tenants who join forces to form a union, or groups of the unemployed and underemployed who organize to get jobs and better wages.

More and more, the civil rights movement will have to engage in the task of organizing people into permanent groups to protect their own interests and produce change in their behalf. This task is tedious, and lacks the drama of demonstrations, but it is necessary for meaningful results.

It is especially important for the Negro middle class to join this action program. To say that all too many members of the Negro middle class have been detached spectators rather than involved participants in the great drama of social change taking place on the stage of American history is not to overlook the unswerving dedication and unselfish service of some. But many middle-class Negroes have forgotten their roots and are more concerned about "conspicuous consumption" than about the cause of justice. Instead, they seek to sit in some serene and passionless realm of isolation, untouched and unmoved by the agonies and struggles of their underprivileged brothers. This kind of selfish detachment has caused the masses of Negroes to feel alienated not only from white society but also from the Negro middle class. They feel that the average middle-class Negro has no concern for their plight.

The feeling is often corroborated by the hard facts of experience. How many Negroes who have achieved educational and economic security have forgotten that they are where they are because of the support of faceless, unlettered and unheralded Negroes who did ordinary jobs in an extraordinary way? How many successful Negroes have forgotten that uneducated and poverty-stricken mothers and fathers often worked until their eyebrows were scorched and their hands bruised so that their children could get an education? For any middle-class Negro to forget the masses is an act not only of neglect but of shameful ingratitude.

It is time for the Negro haves to join hands with the Negro have-nots and, with compassion, journey into that other country of hurt and denial. It is time for the Negro middle class to rise up from its stool of indifference, to retreat from its flight into unreality and to bring its full resources—its heart, its mind and its checkbook—to the aid of the less fortunate brother. The relatively privileged Negro will never be what he ought to be until the underprivileged Negro is what he ought to be. The salvation of the Negro middle class is ultimately dependent upon the salvation of the Negro masses.

A final challenge that we face as a result of our great dilemma is to be ever mindful of enlarging the whole society, and giving it a new sense of values as we seek to solve our particular problem. As we work to get rid of the economic strangulation that we face as a result of poverty, we must not overlook the fact that millions of Puerto Ricans, Mexican Americans, Indians and Appalachian whites are also poverty-stricken. Any serious war against poverty must of necessity include them. As we work to end the educational stagnation that we face as a result of inadequate segregated schools, we must not be unmindful of the fact, as Dr. James Conant has said, the whole public school system is using nineteenth-century educational methods in conditions of twentieth-century urbanization, and that quality education must be enlarged for all children. By and large, the civil rights movement has followed this course, and in so doing has contributed infinitely more to the nation than the eradication of racial injustice. In winning rights for ourselves we have produced substantial benefits for the whole nation.

In the days ahead we must not consider it unpatriotic to raise certain basic questions about our national character. We must begin to ask: Why are there forty million poor people in a nation overflowing with such unbelievable affluence? Why has our nation placed itself in the position of being God's military agent on earth, and intervened recklessly in Vietnam and the Dominican Republic? Why have we substituted the arrogant undertaking of policing the whole world for the high task of putting our own house in order?

All these questions remind us that there is a need for a radical restructuring of the architecture of American society.

For its very survival's sake, America must reexamine old presuppositions and release itself from many things that for centuries have been held sacred. For the evils of racism, poverty and militarism to die, a new set of values must be born. Our economy must become more person-centered than property- and profit-centered. Our government must depend more on its moral power than on its military power.

Let us, therefore, not think of our movement as one that seeks to integrate the Negro into all the existing values of American society. Let us be those creative dissenters who will call our beloved nation to a higher destiny, to a new plateau of compassion, to a more noble expression of humaneness.

We are superbly equipped to do this. We have been seared in the flames of suffering. We have known the agony of being the underdog. We have learned from our have-not status that it profits a nation little to gain the whole world of means and lose the end, its own soul. We must have a passion for peace born out of wretchedness and the misery of war. Giving our ultimate allegiance to the empire of justice, we must be that colony of dissenters seeking to imbue our nation with the ideals of a higher and nobler order. So in dealing with our particular dilemma, we will challenge the nation to deal with its larger dilemma.

This is the challenge. If we will dare to meet it honestly, historians in future years will have to say there lived a great people—a black people—who bore their burdens of oppression in the heat of many days and who, through tenacity and creative commitment, injected new meaning into the veins of American life.

V

Where We Are Going

I

As the administration has manifested a faltering and fluctuating interest in civil rights during the past year, a flood of words rather than deeds has inundated the dry desert of expectations.

One curious explanation of the defaults of the government warrants analysis, because it reveals, without intention, the disadvantages under which the civil rights movement has labored. After describing the obvious—the President's overwhelming preoccupation with the war in Vietnam—it then argues that in 1965 the President was prepared to implement measures leading to full equality but waited in vain for the civil rights movement to offer the programs. The movement is depicted as absorbed in controversy, confused in direction, venal toward its friends and in such turmoil it has tragically lost its golden opportunity to attain change today.

This argument, by explaining everything in terms of the presence or absence of programs, illuminates how the insistence on program can be used as a sophisticated device to evade action. Actually there was no dearth of programs in 1965, ranging from my own proposal, published in 1964, for a Bill of Rights for the Disadvantaged, to elaborate and detailed programs in the published material of many agencies, organizations and individual social scientists. If there had been a sincere disposition seriously to entertain a program, its preparation in final form would have taken but a few weeks. If the federal government had been consumed with fervor to strike an effective blow for civil rights, it need only have begun implementing all the existing laws that are a nullity from one end of the country to the other.

Underneath the invitation to prepare programs is the premise that the government is inherently benevolent—it only awaits presentation of imaginative ideas. When these issue from fertile minds, they will be accepted, enacted and implemented. This premise shifts the burden of responsibility from the white majority, by pretending it is withholding nothing, and places it on the oppressed minority, by pretending the latter is asking for nothing. This is a fable, not a fact. Neither our government nor any government that has sanctioned a century of denial can be depicted as ardent and impatient to bestow gifts of freedom.

When a people are mired in oppression, they realize deliverance when they have accumulated the power to enforce change. When they have amassed such strength, the writing of a program becomes almost an administrative detail. It is immaterial who presents the program; what is material is the presence of an ability to make events happen. The powerful never lose opportunities—they remain available to them. The powerless, on the other hand, never experience opportunity—it is always arriving at a later time.

The deeper truth is that the call to prepare programs distracts us excessively from our basic and primary tasks. If we are seeking a home, there is not much value in discussing blueprints if we have no money and are barred from acquiring the land. We are, in fact, being counseled to put the cart before the horse. We have to put the horse (power) before the cart (programs).

Our nettlesome task is to discover how to organize our strength into compelling power so that government cannot elude our demands. We must develop, from strength, a situation in which the government finds it wise and prudent to collaborate with us. It would be the height of naïveté to wait passively until the administration had somehow been infused with such blessings of goodwill that it implored us for our programs. The first course is grounded in mature realism; the other is childish fantasy.

We do need certain general programs for the movement, but not for use as supplicants. We require programs to hold up to our followers which mirror their aspirations. In this fashion our goals are dramatized and our supporters are inspired to action and to deeper moral commitment.

We must frankly acknowledge that in past years our creativity and imagination were not employed in learning how to develop power. We found a method in nonviolent protest that worked, and we employed it enthusiastically. We did not have leisure to probe for a deeper understanding of its laws and lines of development. Although our actions were bold and crowned with successes, they were substantially improvised and spontaneous. They attained the goals set for them but carried the blemishes of our inexperience.

When a new dawn reveals a landscape dotted with obstacles, the time has come for sober reflection, for assessment of our methods and for anticipating pitfalls. Stumbling and groping through the wilderness finally must be replaced by a planned, organized and orderly march.

None of us can pretend that he knows all the answers. It is enormously difficult for any oppressed people even to arrive at an awareness of their latent strengths. They are not only buffeted by defeats, but they have been schooled assiduously to believe in their lack of capacity. People struggling from the depths of society have not been equipped with knowledge of the science of social change. Only when they break out of the fog of self-denigration can they begin to discover the forms of action that influence events. They can then embark on social experimentation with their own strengths to generate the kind of power that shapes basic decisions.

This is where the civil rights movement stands today. We will err and falter as we climb the unfamiliar slopes of steep mountains, but there is no alternative, well-trod, level path. There will be agonizing setbacks along with creative advances. Our consolation is that no one can know the true taste of victory if he has never swallowed defeat.

For the moment, therefore, we must subordinate programs to studying the levers of power Negroes must grasp to influence the course of events. In our society power sources are sometimes obscure and indistinct. Yet they can always finally be traced to those forces we describe as ideological, economic and political.

In the area of ideology, despite the impact of the works of a few Negro writers on a limited number of white intellectuals, all too few Negro thinkers have exerted an influence on the main currents of American thought. Nevertheless Negroes have illuminated imperfections in the democratic structure that were formerly only dimly perceived, and have forced a concerned reexamination of the true meaning of American democracy. As a consequence of the vigorous Negro protest, the whole nation has for a decade probed more searchingly the essential nature of democracy, both economic and political. By taking to the streets and there giving practical lessons in democracy and its defaults, Negroes have decisively influenced white thought.

Lacking sufficient access to television, publications and broad forums, Negroes have had to write their most persuasive essays with the blunt pen of marching ranks. The many white political leaders and well-meaning friends who ask Negro leadership to leave the streets may not realize that they are asking us effectively to silence ourselves. The twice forgotten man in America has always been the Negro. His groans were not heard, his needs were unfelt, until he found the means to state his case in the public square. More white people learned more about the shame of America, and finally faced some aspects of it, during the years of nonviolent protest than during the century before. Nonviolent direct action will continue to be a significant source of power until it is made irrelevant by the presence of justice.

II

The economic highway to power has few entry lanes for Negroes. Nothing so vividly reveals the crushing impact of discrimination and the heritage of exclusion as the limited dimensions of Negro business in the most powerful economy in the world. America's industrial production is half of the world's total, and within it the production of Negro business is so small that it can scarcely be measured on any definable scale.

Yet in relation to the Negro community the value of Negro business should not be underestimated. In the internal life of the Negro society it provides a degree of stability. Despite formidable obstacles it has developed a corps of men of competence and organizational discipline who constitute a talented leadership reserve. Their cumulative strength may be feeble measured against the mammoth of white industry, but within the community they furnish inspiration and are a resource for the development of programs and planning.

They are a strength among the weak though they are weak among the mighty.

There exist two other areas, however, where Negroes can exert substantial influence on the broader economy. As employees and consumers Negro numbers and their strategic disposition endow them with a certain bargaining strength.

Within the ranks of organized labor there are nearly two million Negroes. Not only are they found in large numbers as workers, but they are concentrated in key industries. In the truck transportation, steel, auto and food industries, which are the backbone of the nation's economic life, Negroes make up nearly 20 percent of the organized work force, although they are only 10 percent of the general population. This potential strength is magnified further by the fact of their unity with millions of white workers in these occupations. As co-workers there is a basic community of interest that transcends many of the ugly divisive elements of traditional prejudice. There are undeniably points of friction, for example, in certain housing and education questions. But the severity of the abrasions is minimized by the more commanding need for cohesion in union organizations.

If manifestations of race prejudice were to erupt within an organized plant, it would set into motion many corrective forces. It would not flourish as it does in a neighborhood with nothing to inhibit it but morbid observers looking for thrills. In the shop the union officials from highest to lowest levels would be immediately involved, for internal discord is no academic matter; it weakens the union in its contests with the employers. Therefore an important self-interest motivates harmonious race relations. Here Negroes have a substantial weight to bring to bear on all measures of social concern.

The labor movement, especially in its earlier days, was one of the few great institutions where a degree of hospitality and mobility was available to Negroes. When the rest of the nation accepted rank discrimination and prejudice as ordinary and usual—like the rain, to be deplored but accepted as part of nature—trade unions, particularly the CIO, leveled all barriers to equal membership. In a number of instances Negroes rose to influential national office.

Today the union record in relation to Negro workers is exceedingly uneven, but the potentiality for influencing union decisions still exists. In many of the larger unions the white leadership contains some men of ideals and many more who are pragmatists. Both groups find they are benefited by a constructive relationship to their Negro membership. For those compelling reasons, Negroes, who are almost wholly a working people, cannot be casual toward the union movement. This is true even though some unions remain incontestably hostile.

In days to come, organized labor will increase its importance in the destinies of Negroes. Automation is imperceptibly but inexorably producing dislocations, skimming off unskilled labor from the industrial force. The displaced are flowing into proliferating service occupations. These enterprises are traditionally unorganized and provide low wage scales with longer hours. The Negroes pressed into these services need union protection, and the union movement needs their membership to maintain its relative strength in the whole society. On this new frontier Negroes may well become the pioneers that they were in the early organizing days of the thirties.

The trade union movement in the last two decades, despite its potential strength, has been an inarticulate giant with an unsteady gait, subjected to abuse and confused in its responses. Some circles of labor, after simmering discontent, are now allowing their challenge to vent itself.

The Teamsters Union, ousted some years ago from the AFL-CIO, instead of tottering or perishing, launched an expansion program that has increased its membership to nearly two million. It is not well known that the Teamsters have well over a quarter of a million Negroes in their ranks, with some of the highest rates of pay enjoyed by Negro workers anywhere in industry. In other mass unions new leaders have emerged with a deep commitment to broad social issues.

Recently, Walter Reuther and other leaders of one and a half million auto workers have announced a new policy directed toward a restoration of the crusading spirit that characterized the unions of the past. They have fashioned a program for organizing the poor, Negro and white, in the South and the North. This will be no simple crusade, because the poor have many problems to overcome even to get into motion. Yet they are so many millions in number that the promise is stirring and its implications are vast.

The emergence of social initiatives by a revitalized labor movement would be taking place as Negroes are placing economic issues on the highest agenda. The coalition of an energized section of labor, Negroes, unemployed and welfare recipients may be the source of power that reshapes economic relationships and ushers in a breakthrough to a new level of social reform. The total elimination of poverty, now a practical possibility, the reality of equality in race relations and other profound structural changes in society may well begin here.

To play our role fully as Negroes we will have to strive for enhanced representation and influence in the labor movement. Our young people need to think of union careers as earnestly as they do of business careers and professions. They could do worse than emulate A. Philip Randolph, who rose to the executive council of the AFL-CIO, and became a symbol of the courage, compassion and integrity of an enlightened labor leader. Indeed, the question may be asked why we have produced only one Randolph in nearly half a century. Discrimination is not the whole answer. We allowed ourselves to accept middle-class prejudices toward the labor movement. Yet this is one of those fields in which higher education is not a requirement for high office. In shunning it, we have lost an opportunity. Let us try to regain it now, at a time when the joint forces of Negro and labor may be facing an historic task of social reform.

The other economic lever available to the Negro is as a consumer. As long ago as 1932, in his book *Moral Man and Immoral Society,* Reinhold Niebuhr pointed out that "boycotts against banks which discriminate against Negroes in quantity credit, against stores which refuse to employ Negroes while serving Negro trade, and against public service corporations which practice racial discrimination, would undoubtedly be crowned with some measure of success."[1] These words have proved to be prophetic, for we have been seeing the success of this approach in the last few years.

SCLC has pioneered in developing mass boycott movements in a frontal attack on discrimination. Our dramatic demonstrations tended to obscure the role of the boycott in cities such as Birmingham. It was not the marching alone that brought about integration of public facilities in 1963. The downtown business establishments suffered for weeks under our almost unbelievably effective boycott. The significant percentage of their sales that vanished, the 98 percent of their Negro customers who stayed home, educated them forcefully to the dignity of the Negro as a consumer.

Later we crystallized our experiences in Birmingham and elsewhere and developed a department in SCLC called Operation Breadbasket. This has as its primary aim the securing of more and better jobs for the Negro people. It calls on the Negro community to support those businesses that will give a fair share of jobs to Negroes and to withdraw its support from those businesses that have discriminatory policies. The key word in Operation Breadbasket is "respect"; it says in substance, "If you respect my dollars, you must respect my person. If you respect my quantitative support, then you must respect the quality of my job and my basic material needs."

Operation Breadbasket is carried out mainly by clergymen. First, a team of ministers calls on the management of a business in the community to request basic facts on the company's total number of employees, the number of Negro employees, the departments or job classifications in which all employees are located, and the salary ranges for each category. The team then returns to the steering committee to evaluate the data and to make a recommendation concerning the number of new and upgraded jobs that should be requested. The decision on the number of jobs requested is usually based on population figures. For instance, if a city has a 30 percent Negro population, then it is logical to assume that Negroes should have at least 30 percent of the jobs in any particular company, and jobs in all categories rather than only in menial areas, as the case almost always happens to be.

The next step is negotiation. The team of clergymen returns to the management of the company and transmits the request to hire or upgrade a specified number of "qualifiable" Negroes within a reasonable period of time. The negotiating sessions are also educational, in that the clergymen seek to arouse within management an awareness of the devastating problems of the ghetto and point out the immorality of companies that make profits from Negro consumers while at the same time excluding them from jobs.

If negotiations break down, the step of real power and pressure is taken. This fourth step consists of a massive call for economic withdrawal from the company's product and accompanying demonstrations if necessary. The ministers go to their pulpits and to other communications media and ask Negroes to stop buying the employer's product or patronizing his business. Clergy-led teams dramatize the dispute to the ghetto inhabitants by picketing the stores where the products in question are sold. The fall-off in trade and the concomitant silencing of the cash register as a result of this boycott is a powerful force in causing the company ultimately to meet the demands.

In most cases it is not necessary to go to step four, because most business executives are keenly aware of the Negro's buying power and the consequent effect of its withdrawal. At present SCLC has Operation Breadbasket functioning in some twelve cities, and the results have been remarkable. In Atlanta, Georgia, for instance, the Negroes' earning power has been increased by more than $20 million annually over the past three years through a carefully disciplined program of selective buying and negotiation by the Negro ministers. During the last eight months in Chicago, Operation Breadbasket successfully completed negotiations with three major industries: milk, soft drinks and chain grocery stores. Four of the companies involved concluded reasonable agreements only after short "don't buy" campaigns. Seven other companies were able to make the requested changes across the conference table, without necessitating a boycott. Two other companies, after providing their employment information to the ministers, were sent letters of commendation for their healthy equal-employment practices. The net results add up to approximately eight hundred new and upgraded jobs for Negro employees, worth a little over $7 million in new annual income for Negro families.

In Chicago we have recently added a new dimension to Operation Breadbasket. Along with requesting new job opportunities, we are now requesting that businesses with stores in the ghetto deposit the income for those establishments in Negro-owned banks, and that Negro-owned products be placed on the counters of all their stores. In this way we seek to stop the drain of resources out of the ghetto with nothing remaining there for its rehabilitation. The two chain grocery stores with which we have so far negotiated, Hi-Low and National Tea, have readily agreed. They have now opened accounts in the two Negro banks of Chicago, and their shelves display every Negro-owned product of the city. This has given new vibrancy and growth to Negro businesses in Chicago, and will contribute to the continued economic growth of the city.

III

The final major area of untapped power for the Negro is in the political arena. Negro population is burgeoning in major cities as tides of migrants flow into them in search of employment and opportunity. These new migrants have substantially higher birth rates than characterize the white population. The two trends, along with the exodus of the white population to the suburbs, are producing fast-gathering Negro majorities in the large cities.

The changing composition of the cities must be seen in the light of their political significance. Particularly in the North, the large cities substantially determine the political destiny of the state. These states, in turn, hold the dominating electoral votes in presidential contests. The future of the

Democratic Party, which rests so heavily on its coalition of urban minorities, cannot be assessed without taking into account which way the Negro vote turns. The wistful hopes of the Republican Party for large city influence will also be decided not in the boardrooms of great corporations but in the teeming ghettos. Its 1964 disaster with Goldwater, in which fewer than 6 percent of Negroes voted Republican, indicates that the illustrious ghost of Abraham Lincoln is not sufficient for winning Negro confidence, not so long as the party fails to shrink the influence of its ultra-right wing.

The growing Negro vote in the South is another source of power. As it weakens and enfeebles the Dixiecrats, by concentrating its blows against them, it undermines the congressional coalition of Southern reactionaries and their Northern Republican colleagues. That coalition, which has always exercised a disproportionate power in Congress by controlling its major committees, will lose its ability to frustrate measures of social advancement and to impose its perverted definition of democracy on the political thought of the nation.

The Negro vote presently is only a partially realized strength. It can still be doubled in the South. In the North, even where Negroes are registered in equal proportion to whites, they do not vote in the same proportions. Assailed by a sense of futility, Negroes resist participating in empty ritual. However, when the Negro citizen learns that united and organized pressure can achieve measurable results, he will make his influence felt. Out of this consciousness the political power of the aroused minority will be enhanced and consolidated.

Up to now that power has been inconsequential because, paradoxically, although Negroes vote with great discernment and traditionally as a bloc, essentially we are unorganized, disunited and subordinated in the decision-making process.

There is no correlation between the numerical importance of the urban Negro vote to the party it supports and the influence we wield in determining the party's program and policies, or its implementation of existing legislation. Our political leaders are bereft of influence in the councils of political power.

The new task of the liberation movement, therefore, is not merely to increase the Negro registration and vote; equally imperative is the development of a strong voice that is heard in the smoke-filled rooms where party debating and bargaining proceed. A black face that is mute in party councils is not political representation; the ability to be independent, assertive and respected when the final decisions are made is indispensable for an authentic expression of power.

Negroes are traditionally manipulated because the political powers take advantage of three major weaknesses. The first relates to the manner in which our political leaders emerge; the second is our failure so far to achieve effective political alliances; the third is the Negro's general reluctance to participate fully in political life.

The majority of Negro political leaders do not ascend to prominence on the shoulders of mass support. Although genuinely popular leaders are now emerging, most are selected by white leadership, elevated to position, supplied with resources and inevitably subjected to white control. The mass of Negroes nurtures a healthy suspicion toward these manufactured leaders. Experience tells them that color is the chief argument their leaders are offering to induce loyalty and solidarity. The Negro politician they know spends little time in persuading them that he embodies personal integrity, commitment and ability; he offers few programs and less service. Tragically, he is in too many respects not a fighter for a new life but a figurehead of the old one. Hence very few

Negro political leaders are impressive or illustrious to their constituents. They enjoy only limited loyalty and qualified support.

This relationship in turn hampers the Negro leader in bargaining with genuine strength and independent firmness with white party leaders. The whites are all too well aware of his impotence and his remoteness from his constituents, and they deal with him as a powerless subordinate. He is accorded a measure of dignity and personal respect but not political power.

The Negro politician therefore finds himself in a vacuum. He has no base in either direction on which to build influence and attain leverage.

In Negro life there is a unique and unnatural dichotomy between community leaders who have the respect of the masses and professional political leaders who are held in polite disdain. Those who lead civil rights groups, churches, unions and other social organizations are actually hybrids; although they bargain for political programs, they generally operate outside of partisan politics. In two national polls[2] to name the most respected Negro leaders, out of the highest fifteen, only a single political figure, Congressman Adam Clayton Powell, was included and he was in the lower half of both lists. This is in marked contrast to polls in which white people choose their most popular leaders; political personalities are always high on the lists and are represented in goodly numbers. There is no Negro political personality evoking affection, respect and emulation to correspond to John F. Kennedy, Eleanor Roosevelt, Herbert Lehman, Earl Warren and Adlai Stevenson, to name but a few.

The circumstances in which Congressman Powell emerged into leadership and the experiences of his career are unique. It would not shed light on the larger picture to attempt to study the very individual factors that apply to him. It is fair to say no other Negro political leader is similar, either in the strengths he possesses, the power he attained or the errors he has committed.

And so we shall have to do more than register and more than vote; we shall have to create leaders who embody virtues we can respect, who have moral and ethical principles we can applaud with an enthusiasm that enables us to rally support for them based on confidence and trust. We will have to demand high standards and give consistent, loyal support to those who merit it. We will have to be a reliable constituency for those who prove themselves to be committed political warriors in our behalf. When our movement has partisan political personalities whose unity with their people is unshakable and whose independence is genuine, they will be treated in white political councils with the respect those who embody such power deserve.

In addition to the development of genuinely independent and representative political leaders, we shall have to master the art of political alliances. Negroes should be natural allies of many white reform and independent political groups, yet they are more commonly organized by old-line machine politicians. We will have to learn to refuse crumbs from the big-city machines and steadfastly demand a fair share of the loaf. When the machine politicians demur, we must be prepared to act in unity and throw our support to such independent parties or reform wings of the major parties as are prepared to take our demands seriously and fight for them vigorously. This is political freedom; this is political maturity expressing our aroused and determined new spirit to be treated as equals in all aspects of life.

The future of the deep structural changes we seek will not

be found in the decaying political machines. It lies in new alliances of Negroes, Puerto Ricans, labor, liberals, certain church and middle-class elements. It is noteworthy that the largest single civil rights action ever conducted was the New York school boycott, when nearly half a million Negroes and Puerto Ricans united in a demonstration that emptied segregated schools.

The art of alliance politics is more complex and more intricate than it is generally pictured. It is easy to put exciting combinations on paper. It evokes happy memories to recall that our victories in the past decade were won with a broad coalition of organizations representing a wide variety of interests. But we deceive ourselves if we envision the same combination backing structural changes in the society. It did not come together for such a program and will not reassemble for it.

A true alliance is based upon some self-interest of each component group and a common interest into which they merge. For an alliance to have permanence and loyal commitment from its various elements, each of them must have a goal from which it benefits and none must have an outlook in basic conflict with the others. Thus we cannot talk loosely of an alliance with all labor. Most unions have mutual interests with us; both can profit in the relationship. Yet with some unions that persist in discrimination to retain their monopoly of jobs we have no common ground. To talk of alliances with them is to talk of mutual deception and mutual hypocrisy. The same test must be applied to churches and church bodies. Some churches recognize that to be relevant in moral life they must make equality an imperative. With them the basis for alliance is strong and enduring. But toward those churches that shun and evade the issue, that are mute or timorous on social and economic questions, we are no better than strangers even though we sing the same hymns in worship of the same God.

If we employ the principle of selectivity along these lines, we will find millions of allies who in serving themselves also support us, and on such sound foundations unity and mutual trust and tangible accomplishment will flourish.

It is no mere academic exercise to scrutinize alliance relationships. They are the keys to political progress. Of late some scholars have begun to question the usefulness of the Negro vote as a tool for social advancement. Matthews and Prothro put it "that the concrete benefits to be derived from the franchise—under the conditions that prevail in the South— have often been exaggerated. . . . The concrete, measurable payoffs from Negro voting in the South will *not* be revolutionary."[3] They point to the limited gains Negroes have attained in the North and apply them to the South. Their conclusion has some validity because they confine them to conditions that *prevail* in the South. But conditions in the South are not static; they are changing.

A primary Negro political goal in the South is the elimination of racism as an electoral issue. No objective observer can fail to see that even with a half-finished campaign to enfranchise Negroes some profound changes have already occurred. For a number of years there were de facto alliances in some states in which Negroes voted for the same candidate as whites because he had shifted from a racist to a moderate position, even though he did not articulate an appeal for Negro votes. In recent years the transformation has accelerated, and many white candidates have entered alliances publicly. As they perceived that the Negro vote was becoming a substantial and permanent factor, they could not remain aloof from it. More and more, competition will develop among white political forces for such a significant bloc of votes, and a monolithic white unity based on racism will no longer be possible.

Racism is a tenacious evil, but it is not immutable. Millions of underprivileged whites are in the process of considering the contradiction between segregation and economic progress. White supremacy can feed their egos but not their stomachs. They will not go hungry or forego the affluent society to remain racially ascendant. Governors [George] Wallace and [Lester] Maddox, whose credentials as racists are impeccable, understand this, and for that reason they present themselves as liberal populists as well. Their demagoguery is little known to Northerners, who have no opportunity to hear the speeches they make in local communities. Temporarily they can carry water on both shoulders, but the ground is becoming unsteady beneath their feet. Each of them was faced in the primary with a new breed of white Southerner. Their opponents were not inconsequential political figures. Former governors were in the race, making open public appeals for the Negro vote and for the first time in history meeting with Negro organizations to solicit support. They championed economic reform without racial demagoguery. They won significant numbers of white votes, insufficient for victory but sufficient to point the future directions of the South.

The time may not be far off when an awakened poor and backward white voter will heed and support the authentic economic liberalism of former governor [Ellis] Arnall of Georgia and former lieutenant governor [Richmond] Flowers of Alabama. Then with the growing Negro vote they will develop an alliance that displaces the Wallaces and with them racism as a political issue.

It is true that the Negro vote has not transformed the

North; but the fact that Northern alliances and political action generally have been poorly executed is no reason to predict that the negative experiences will be automatically extended in the North or duplicated in the South. The Northern Negro has never used direct action on a mass scale for reforms, and anyone who predicted ten years ago that the Southern Negro would also neglect it would have dramatically been proved in error.

Everything Negroes need—and many of us need almost everything—will not like magic materialize from the use of the ballot. Yet as a lever of power, if it is given studious attention and employed with the creativity we have proved through our protest activities we possess, it will help to achieve many far-reaching changes during our lifetimes.

The final reason for our dearth of political strength, particularly in the North, arises from the grip of an old tradition on many individual Negroes. They tend to hold themselves aloof from politics as a serious concern. They sense that they are manipulated, and their defense is a cynical disinterest. To safeguard themselves on this front from the exploitation that torments them in so many areas, they shut the door to political activity and retreat into the dark shadows of passivity. Their sense of futility is deep, and in terms of their bitter experiences it is justified. They cannot perceive political action as a source of power. It will take patient and persistent effort to eradicate this mood, but the new consciousness of strength developed in a decade of stirring agitation can be utilized to channel constructive Negro activity into political life and eliminate the stagnation produced by an outdated and defensive paralysis.

In the future we must become intensive political activists. We must be guided in this direction because we need political strength more desperately than any other group in

American society. Most of us are too poor to have adequate, economic power, and many of us are too rejected by the culture to be part of any tradition of power. Necessity will draw us toward the power inherent in the creative uses of politics.

Negroes nurture a persisting myth that the Jews of America attained social mobility and status solely because they had money. It is unwise to ignore the error for many reasons. In a negative sense it encourages anti-Semitism and overestimates money as a value. In a positive sense the full truth reveals a useful lesson.

Jews progressed because they possessed a tradition of education combined with social and political action. The Jewish family enthroned education and sacrificed to get it. The result was far more than abstract learning. Uniting social action with educational competence, Jews became enormously effective in political life. Those Jews who became lawyers, businessmen, writers, entertainers, union leaders and medical men did not vanish into the pursuits of their trade exclusively. They lived an active life in political circles, learning the techniques and arts of politics.

Nor was it only the rich who were involved in social and political action. Millions of Jews for half a century remained relatively poor, but they were far from passive in social and political areas. They lived in homes in which politics was a household word. They were deeply involved in radical parties, liberal parties and conservative parties—they formed many of them. Very few Jews sank into despair and escapism even when discrimination assailed the spirit and corroded initiative. Their life raft in the sea of discouragement was social action.

Without overlooking the towering differences between the Negro and Jewish experiences, the lesson of Jewish mass involvement in social and political action and education is worthy of emulation. Negroes have already started on this road in creating the protest movement, but this is only a beginning. We must involve everyone we can reach, even those with inadequate education, and together acquire political sophistication by discussion, practice and reading. Jews without education learned a great deal from political meetings, mass meetings and trade union activities. Informal discussions and reading at home or in the streets are educational; they challenge the mind and inform our actions.

Education without social action is a one-sided value because it has no true power potential. Social action without education is a weak expression of pure energy. Deeds uninformed by educated thought can take false directions. When we go into action and confront our adversaries, we must be as armed with knowledge as they. Our policies should have the strength of deep analysis beneath them to be able to challenge the clever sophistries of our opponents.

The many thousands of Negroes who have already found intellectual growth and spiritual fulfillment on this path know its creative possibilities. They are not among the legions of the lost, they are not crushed by the weight of centuries. Most heartening, among the young the spirit of challenge and determination for change is becoming an unquenchable force.

But the scope of struggle is still too narrow and too restricted. We must turn more of our energies and focus our creativity on the useful things that translate into power. This is not a program for a distant tomorrow, when our children will somehow have acquired enough education to do it for themselves. We in this generation must do the work and in doing it stimulate our children to learn and acquire higher levels of skill and technique.

It must become a crusade so vital that civil rights organizers do not repeatedly have to make personal calls to summon support. There must be a climate of social pressure in the Negro community that scorns the Negro who will not pick up his citizenship rights and add his strength enthusiastically and voluntarily to the accumulation of power for himself and his people. The past years have blown fresh winds through ghetto stagnation, but we are on the threshold of a significant change that demands a hundredfold acceleration. By 1970 ten of our larger cities will have Negro majorities if present trends continue. We can shrug off this opportunity or use it for a new vitality to deepen and enrich our family and community life.

How shall we turn the ghettos into a vast school? How shall we make every street corner a forum, not a lounging place for trivial gossip and petty gambling, where life is wasted and human experience withers to trivial sensations? How shall we make every houseworker and every laborer a demonstrator, a voter, a canvasser and a student? The dignity their jobs may deny them is waiting for them in political and social action.

We must utilize the community action groups and training centers now proliferating in some slum areas to create not merely an electorate, but a conscious, alert and informed people who know their direction and whose collective wisdom and vitality commands respect. The slave heritage can be cast into the dim past by our consciousness of our strengths and a resolute determination to use them in our daily experiences. Power is not the white man's birthright; it will not be legislated for us and delivered in neat government packages. It is a social force any group can utilize by accumulating its elements in a planned, deliberate campaign to organize it under its own control.

IV

While the existence of a militant morale is immensely important, a fighting spirit that is insufficiently organized can become useless and even hazardous. To attempt radical reform without adequate organization is like trying to sail a boat without a rudder. Yet any mature analysis of recent events cannot fail to recognize the frailties of Negro civil rights organizations.

Prominent among the significant weaknesses of our organizations is their disunity and petty competition. When false rumors are circulated that some leaders have "sold out" to the power structure or are making opportunistic alliances with one or another political party to gain individual advantage, the whole movement suffers. If the criticism is true, it is not destructive; it is a necessary attack on weakness. But often such criticism is a reflex response to gain organizational advantage. Too often a genuine achievement has been falsely condemned as spurious and useless, and a victory has been turned into disheartening defeat for the less informed. Our enemies will adequately deflate our accomplishment; we need not serve them as eager volunteers.

Why are so many of our organizations too small, too beset with problems that consume disproportionate attention, or too dominated by a sluggish passivity and smug complacency? For an answer we must return to the nature of our original objectives. For much of the last decade we took on the task of ending conditions that had long outlived their purpose. The desegregation of most public facilities, for example, was overdue for change. It was not necessary to build a widespread organization in order to win legislative victories. Sound effort in a single city such as Birmingham or Selma produced situations that symbolized the evil everywhere and inflamed public opinion against it. Where the spotlight illuminated the evil, a legislative remedy was soon obtained that applied everywhere. As a consequence, permanent, seasoned and militant organizations did not arise out of compelling necessity.

But corrective legislation requires organization to bring it to life. Laws only declare rights; they do not deliver them. The oppressed must take hold of laws and transform them into effective mandates. Hence the absence of powerful organization has limited the degree of application and the extent of practical success.

We made easy gains and we built the kind of organizations that expect easy victories, and rest upon them. It may seem curious to speak of easy victories when some have suffered and sacrificed so much. Yet in candor and self-criticism it is necessary to acknowledge that the tortuous job of organizing solidly and simultaneously in thousands of places was not a feature of our work. This is as true for the older civil rights organizations as for the newer ones. The older organizations have only acquired a mass base recently, and they still retain the flabby structures and policies that a pressureless situation made possible.

Many civil rights organizations were born as specialists in agitation and dramatic projects; they attracted massive sympathy and support; but they did not assemble and unify the support for new stages of struggle. The effect on their allies reflected their basic practices. Support waxed and waned, and people became conditioned to action in crises but inaction from day to day. We unconsciously patterned a crisis policy and program, and summoned support not for daily commitment but for explosive events alone.

Recognizing that no army can mobilize and demobilize and remain a fighting unit, we will have to build far-flung, workmanlike and experienced organizations in the future if the legislation we create and the agreements we forge are to be ably and zealously superintended. Moreover, to move to higher levels of progress we will have to emerge from crises with more than agreements and laws. We shall have to have people tied together in a long-term relationship instead of evanescent enthusiasts who lose their experience, spirit and unity because they have no mechanism that directs them to new tasks.

We have many assets to facilitate organization. Negroes are almost instinctively cohesive. We band together readily, and against white hostility we have an intense and wholesome loyalty to each other. In some of the simplest relationships we will protect a brother even at a cost to ourselves. We are loath to be witnesses against each other when the white man seeks to divide us. We are acutely conscious of the need and sharply sensitive to the importance of defending our own. Solidarity is a reality in Negro life, as it always has been among the oppressed. Sometimes, unfortunately, it is misapplied when we confuse high status with high character.

On the other hand, Negroes are capable of becoming competitive, carping and, in an expression of self-hate, suspicious and intolerant of each other. A glaring weakness in Negro life is lack of sufficient mutual confidence and trust.

Negro leaders suffer from this interplay of solidarity and divisiveness, being either exalted excessively or grossly abused. But some of those leaders who suffer from lack of sustained support are not without weaknesses that give substance to criticism. The most serious is aloofness and absence of faith in their people. The white establishment is skilled in flattering and cultivating emerging leaders. It presses its own image on them and finally, from imitation of manners, dress and style of living, a deeper strain of corruption develops. This kind of Negro leader acquires the white man's contempt for the ordinary Negro. He is often more at home with the middle-class white than he is among his own people, and frequently his physical home is moved up and away from the ghetto. His language changes, his location changes, his income changes, and ultimately he changes from the representative of the Negro to the white man into the white man's representative to the Negro. The tragedy is that too often he does not recognize what has happened to him.

I learned a lesson many years ago from a report of two men who flew to Atlanta to confer with a civil rights leader at the airport. Before they could begin to talk, the porter sweeping the floor drew the local leader aside to talk about a matter that troubled him. After fifteen minutes had passed, one of the visitors said bitterly to his companion, "I am just too busy for this kind of nonsense. I haven't come a thousand miles to sit and wait while he talks to a porter."

The other replied, "When the day comes that he stops having time to talk to a porter, on that day I will not have the time to come one mile to see him."

When I heard this story, I knew I was being told something I should never forget.

We need organizations that are permeated with mutual trust, incorruptibility and militancy. Without this spirit we may have numbers but they will add up to zero. We need organizations that are responsible, efficient and alert. We lack experience because ours is a history of disorganization. But we will prevail because our need for progress is stronger than the ignorance forced upon us. If we realize how indispensable is responsible militant organization to our struggle, we will create it as we managed to create underground railroads, protest groups, self-help societies and the churches that have always been our refuge, our source of hope and our source of action.

V

In recent years a multitude of civil rights programs have been elicited from specialists and scholars. To enhance their value and increase support for them, it is necessary that they be discussed and debated among the ordinary people affected by them. To facilitate study, I have grouped some of the more challenging proposals separately in an appendix to this volume. There is only one general proposal that I would like to examine here, because it deals with the abolition of poverty within this nation and leads logically to my final discussion of poverty on an international scale.

In the treatment of poverty nationally, one fact stands out: there are twice as many white poor as Negro poor in the United States. Therefore I will not dwell on the experiences of poverty that derive from racial discrimination, but will discuss the poverty that affects white and Negro alike.

Up to recently we have proceeded from a premise that poverty is a consequence of multiple evils: lack of education restricting job opportunities; poor housing which stultified home life and suppressed initiative; fragile family relationships which distorted personality development. The logic of this approach suggested that each of these causes be attacked one by one. Hence a housing program to transform living conditions, improved educational facilities to furnish tools for better job opportunities, and family counseling to create better personal adjustments were designed. In combination these measures were intended to remove the causes of poverty.

While none of these remedies in itself is unsound, all have a fatal disadvantage. The programs have never proceeded on a coordinated basis or at similar rates of development. Housing measures have fluctuated at the whims of legislative bodies. They have been piecemeal and pygmy. Educational reforms have been even more sluggish and entangled in bureaucratic stalling and economy-dominated decisions. Family assistance stagnated in neglect and then suddenly was discovered to be the central issue on the basis of hasty and superficial studies. At no time has a total, coordinated and fully adequate program been conceived. As a consequence, fragmentary and spasmodic reforms have failed to reach down to the profoundest needs of the poor.

In addition to the absence of coordination and sufficiency, the programs of the past all have another common failing—they are indirect. Each seeks to solve poverty by first solving something else.

I am now convinced that the simplest approach will prove to be the most effective—the solution to poverty is to abolish it directly by a now widely discussed measure: the guaranteed income.

Earlier in this century this proposal would have been greeted with ridicule and denunciation as destructive of initiative and responsibility. At that time economic status was considered the measure of the individual's abilities and talents. In the simplistic thinking of that day the absence of worldly goods indicated a want of industrious habits and moral fiber.

We have come a long way in our understanding of human motivation and of the blind operation of our economic system. Now we realize that dislocations in the market operation of our economy and the prevalence of discrimination thrust people into idleness and bind them in constant or frequent unemployment against their will. The poor are less often dismissed from our conscience today by being branded as inferior and incompetent. We also know that no matter how dynamically the economy develops and expands it does not eliminate all poverty.

We have come to the point where we must make the nonproducer a consumer or we will find ourselves drowning in a sea of consumer goods. We have so energetically mastered production that we now must give attention to distribution. Though there have been increases in purchasing power, they have lagged behind increases in production. Those at the lowest economic level, the poor white and Negro, the aged and chronically ill, are traditionally unorganized and therefore have little ability to force the necessary growth in their income. They stagnate or become even poorer in relation to the larger society.

The problem indicates that our emphasis must be twofold. We must create full employment or we must create incomes. People must be made consumers by one method or the other. Once they are placed in this position, we need to be concerned that the potential of the individual is not wasted. New forms of work that enhance the social good will have to be devised for those for whom traditional jobs are not available.

In 1879 Henry George anticipated this state of affairs when he wrote, in *Progress and Poverty:*

> The fact is that the work which improves the condition of mankind, the work which extends knowledge and increases power and enriches literature, and elevates thought, is not done to secure a living. It is not the work of slaves, driven to their task either by the lash of a master or by animal necessities. It is the work

of men who perform it for their own sake, and not that they may get more to eat or drink, or wear, or display. In a state of society where want is abolished, work of this sort could be enormously increased.

We are likely to find that the problems of housing and education, instead of preceding the elimination of poverty, will themselves be affected if poverty is first abolished. The poor transformed into purchasers will do a great deal on their own to alter housing decay. Negroes, who have a double disability, will have a greater effect on discrimination when they have the additional weapon of cash to use in their struggle.

Beyond these advantages, a host of positive psychological changes inevitably will result from widespread economic security. The dignity of the individual will flourish when the decisions concerning his life are in his own hands, when he has the assurance that his income is stable and certain, and when he knows that he has the means to seek self improvement. Personal conflicts between husband, wife and children will diminish when the unjust measurement of human worth on a scale of dollars is eliminated.

Two conditions are indispensable if we are to ensure that the guaranteed income operates as a consistently progressive measure. First, it must be pegged to the median income of society, not at the lowest levels of income. To guarantee an income at the floor would simply perpetuate welfare standards and freeze into the society poverty conditions. Second, the guaranteed income must be dynamic; it must automatically increase as the total social income grows. Were it permitted to remain static under growth conditions, the recipients would suffer a relative decline. If periodic reviews disclose that the whole national income has risen, then the guaranteed income would have to be adjusted upward by the same percentage. Without these safeguards a creeping retrogression would occur, nullifying the gains of security and stability.

This proposal is not a "civil rights" program, in the sense that that term is currently used. The program would benefit all the poor, including the two-thirds of them who are white. I hope that both Negro and white will act in coalition to effect this change, because their combined strength will be necessary to overcome the fierce opposition we must realistically anticipate.

Our nation's adjustment to a new mode of thinking will be facilitated if we realize that for nearly forty years two groups in our society have already been enjoying a guaranteed income. Indeed, it is a symptom of our confused social values that these two groups turn out to be the richest and the poorest. The wealthy who own securities have always had an assured income; and their polar opposite, the relief client, has been guaranteed an income, however minuscule, through welfare benefits.

John Kenneth Galbraith has estimated that $20 billion a year would effect a guaranteed income, which he describes as "not much more than we will spend the next fiscal year to rescue freedom and democracy and religious liberty as these are defined by 'experts' in Vietnam."[4]

The contemporary tendency in our society is to base our distribution on scarcity, which has vanished, and to compress our abundance into the overfed mouths of the middle and upper classes until they gag with superfluity. If democracy is to have breadth of meaning, it is necessary to adjust this inequity. It is not only moral, but it is also intelligent. We are wasting and degrading human life by clinging to archaic thinking.

The curse of poverty has no justification in our age. It is socially as cruel and blind as the practice of cannibalism at the dawn of civilization, when men ate each other because they had not yet learned to take food from the soil or to consume the abundant animal life around them. The time has come for us to civilize ourselves by the total, direct and immediate abolition of poverty.

VI

The World House

S ome years ago a famous novelist died. Among his pa-
pers was found a list of suggested plots for future stories,
the most prominently underscored being this one: "A
widely separated family inherits a house in which they have
to live together." This is the great new problem of mankind.
We have inherited a large house, a great "world house" in
which we have to live together—black and white, Easterner
and Westerner, Gentile and Jew, Catholic and Protestant,
Muslim and Hindu—a family unduly separated in ideas, culture and interest, who, because we can never again live apart,
must learn somehow to live with each other in peace.

However deeply American Negroes are caught in the
struggle to be at last at home in our homeland of the United
States, we cannot ignore the larger world house in which
we are also dwellers. Equality with whites will not solve the
problems of either whites or Negroes if it means equality in a
world society stricken by poverty and in a universe doomed
to extinction by war.

All inhabitants of the globe are now neighbors. This
worldwide neighborhood has been brought into being
largely as a result of the modern scientific and technological
revolutions. The world of today is vastly different from the

world of just one hundred years ago. A century ago Thomas Edison had not yet invented the incandescent lamp to bring light to many dark places of the earth. The Wright brothers had not yet invented that fascinating mechanical bird that would spread its gigantic wings across the skies and soon dwarf distance and place time in the service of man. Einstein had not yet challenged an axiom and the theory of relativity had not yet been posited.

Human beings, searching a century ago as now for better understanding, had no television, no radios, no telephones and no motion pictures through which to communicate. Medical science had not yet discovered the wonder drugs to end many dread plagues and diseases. One hundred years ago military men had not yet developed the terrifying weapons of warfare that we know today—not the bomber, an airborne fortress raining down death; nor napalm, that burner of all things and flesh in its path. A century ago there were no sky-scraping buildings to kiss the stars and no gargantuan bridges to span the waters. Science had not yet peered into the unfathomable ranges of interstellar space, nor had it penetrated oceanic depths. All these new inventions, these new ideas, these sometimes fascinating and sometimes frightening developments, came later. Most of them have come within the past sixty years, sometimes with agonizing slowness, more characteristically with bewildering speed, but always with enormous significance for our future.

The years ahead will see a continuation of the same dramatic developments. Physical science will carve new highways through the stratosphere. In a few years astronauts and cosmonauts will probably walk comfortably across the uncertain pathways of the moon. In two or three years it will be possible, because of the new supersonic jets, to fly from New York to London in two and one-half hours. In the years ahead medical science will greatly prolong the lives of men by finding a cure for cancer and deadly heart ailments. Automation and cybernation will make it possible for working people to have undreamed-of amounts of leisure time. All this is a dazzling picture of the furniture, the workshop, the spacious rooms, the new decorations and the architectural pattern of the large world house in which we are living.

Along with the scientific and technological revolution, we have also witnessed a worldwide freedom revolution over the last few decades. The present upsurge of the Negro people of the United States grows out of a deep and passionate determination to make freedom and equality a reality "here" and "now." In one sense the civil rights movement in the United States is a special American phenomenon which must be understood in the light of American history and dealt with in terms of the American situation. But on another and more important level, what is happening in the United States today is a significant part of a world development.

We live in a day, said the philosopher Alfred North Whitehead, "when civilization is shifting its basic outlook; a major turning point in history where the pre-suppositions on which society is structured are being analyzed, sharply challenged, and profoundly changed." What we are seeing now is a freedom explosion, the realization of "an idea whose time has come," to use Victor Hugo's phrase. The deep rumbling of discontent that we hear today is the thunder of disinherited masses, rising from dungeons of oppression to the bright hills of freedom. In one majestic chorus the rising masses are singing, in the words of our freedom song, "Ain't gonna let nobody turn us around." All over the world like a fever, freedom is spreading in the widest liberation movement in history. The great masses of people are determined to end the exploitation of their races and lands. They are awake and moving toward their goal like a tidal wave. You can hear them rumbling in every village street, on the docks, in the houses, among the students, in the churches and at political meetings. For several centuries the direction of history flowed from the nations and societies of Western Europe out into the rest of the world in "conquests" of various sorts. That period, the era of colonialism, is at an end. East is moving West. The earth is being redistributed. Yes, we are "shifting our basic outlooks."

These developments should not surprise any student of history. Oppressed people cannot remain oppressed forever. The yearning for freedom eventually manifests itself. The Bible tells the thrilling story of how Moses stood in Pharaoh's court centuries ago and cried, "Let my people go." This was an opening chapter in a continuing story. The present struggle in the United States is a later chapter in the same story. Something within has reminded the Negro of his birthright of freedom, and something without has reminded him that it can be gained. Consciously or unconsciously, he has been caught up by the spirit of the times, and with his black brothers of Africa and his brown and yellow brothers in Asia, South America and the Caribbean, the United States Negro is moving with a sense of great urgency toward the promised land of racial justice.

Nothing could be more tragic than for men to live in these revolutionary times and fail to achieve the new attitudes and the new mental outlooks that the new situation demands. In Washington Irving's familiar story of Rip Van Winkle, the one thing that we usually remember is that Rip slept twenty years. There is another important point, however, that is almost always overlooked. It was the sign on the inn in the little town on the Hudson from which Rip departed and scaled the mountain for his long sleep. When he went up, the sign had a picture of King George III of England. When he came down, twenty years later, the sign had a picture of George Washington. As he looked at the picture of the first President of the United States, Rip was confused, flustered and lost. He knew not who Washington was. The most striking thing about this story is not that Rip slept twenty years, but that he slept through a revolution that would alter the course of human history.

One of the great liabilities of history is that all too many people fail to remain awake through great periods of social change. Every society has its protectors of the status quo and its fraternities of the indifferent who are notorious for sleeping through revolutions. But today our very survival depends on our ability to stay awake, to adjust to new ideas, to remain vigilant and to face the challenge of change. The large house in which we live demands that we transform this worldwide neighborhood into a worldwide brotherhood. Together we must learn to live as brothers or together we will be forced to perish as fools.

We must work passionately and indefatigably to bridge the gulf between our scientific progress and our moral progress. One of the great problems of mankind is that we suffer from a poverty of the spirit which stands in glaring contrast to our scientific and technological abundance. The richer we have become materially, the poorer we have become morally and spiritually.

Every man lives in two realms, the internal and the external. The internal is that realm of spiritual ends expressed in art, literature, morals and religion. The external is that complex of devices, techniques, mechanisms and instrumentalities by means of which we live. Our problem today is that we have allowed the internal to become lost in the external. We have allowed the means by which we live to outdistance the ends for which we live. So much of modern life can be summarized in that suggestive phrase of Thoreau: "Improved means to an unimproved end." This is the serious predicament, the deep and haunting problem, confronting modern man. Enlarged material powers spell enlarged peril if there is not proportionate growth of the soul. When the external of man's nature subjugates the internal, dark storm clouds begin to form.

Western civilization is particularly vulnerable at this moment, for our material abundance has brought us neither peace of mind nor serenity of spirit. An Asian writer has portrayed our dilemma in candid terms:

> You call your thousand material devices "labor-saving machinery," yet you are forever "busy." With the multiplying of your machinery you grow increasingly fatigued, anxious, nervous, dissatisfied. Whatever you have, you want more; and wherever you are you want to go somewhere else . . . your devices are neither time-saving nor soul-saving machinery. They are so many sharp spurs which urge you on to invent more machinery and to do more business.[1]

This tells us something about our civilization that cannot be cast aside as a prejudiced charge by an Eastern thinker who is jealous of Western prosperity. We cannot escape the indictment.

This does not mean that we must turn back the clock of scientific progress. No one can overlook the wonders that science has wrought for our lives. The automobile will not abdicate in favor of the horse and buggy, or the train in favor of the stagecoach, or the tractor in favor of the hand plow, or the scientific method in favor of ignorance and superstition. But our moral and spiritual "lag" must be redeemed.

When scientific power outruns moral power, we end up with guided missiles and misguided men. When we foolishly minimize the internal of our lives and maximize the external, we sign the warrant for our own day of doom.

Our hope for creative living in this world house that we have inherited lies in our ability to reestablish the moral ends of our lives in personal character and social justice. Without this spiritual and moral reawakening we shall destroy ourselves in the misuse of our own instruments.

II

Among the moral imperatives of our time, we are challenged to work all over the world with unshakable determination to wipe out the last vestiges of racism. As early as 1906 W. E. B. Du Bois prophesied that "the problem of the twentieth century will be the problem of the color line." Now as we stand two-thirds into this exciting period of history we know full well that racism is still that hound of hell which dogs the tracks of our civilization.

Racism is no mere American phenomenon. Its vicious grasp knows no geographical boundaries. In fact, racism and its perennial ally—economic exploitation—provide the key to understanding most of the international complications of this generation.

The classic example of organized and institutionalized racism is the Union of South Africa. Its national policy and practice are the incarnation of the doctrine of white supremacy in the midst of a population which is overwhelmingly black. But the tragedy of South Africa is not simply in its own policy; it is the fact that the racist government of South Africa is virtually made possible by the economic policies of the United States and Great Britain, two countries which profess to be the moral bastions of our Western world.

In country after country we see white men building empires on the sweat and suffering of colored people. Portu-
gal continues its practices of slave labor and subjugation in
Angola; the Ian Smith government in Rhodesia continues
to enjoy the support of British-based industry and private
capital, despite the stated opposition of British government
policy. Even in the case of the little country of South West
Africa we find the powerful nations of the world incapable
of taking a moral position against South Africa, though the
smaller country is under the trusteeship of the United Nations. Its policies are controlled by South Africa and its manpower is lured into the mines under slave-labor conditions.

During the Kennedy administration there was some
awareness of the problems that breed in the racist and exploitative conditions throughout the colored world, and a
temporary concern emerged to free the United States from
its complicity though the effort was only on a diplomatic
level. Through our ambassador to the United Nations, Adlai Stevenson, there emerged the beginnings of an intelligent
approach to the colored peoples of the world. However,
there remained little or no attempt to deal with the economic aspects of racist exploitation. We have been notori-
ously silent about the more than $700 million of American
capital which props up the system of apartheid, not to mention the billions of dollars in trade and the military alliances
which are maintained under the pretext of fighting Communism in Africa.

Nothing provides the Communists with a better climate
for expansion and infiltration than the continued alliance
of our nation with racism and exploitation throughout the
world. And if we are not diligent in our determination to
root out the last vestiges of racism in our dealings with the
rest of the world, we may soon see the sins of our fathers

visited upon ours and succeeding generations. For the conditions which are so classically represented in Africa are present also in Asia and in our own back yard in Latin America.

Everywhere in Latin America one finds a tremendous resentment of the United States, and that resentment is always strongest among the poorer and darker peoples of the continent. The life and destiny of Latin America are in the hands of United States corporations. The decisions affecting the lives of South Americans are ostensibly made by their government, but there are almost no legitimate democracies alive in the whole continent. The other governments are dominated by huge and exploitative cartels that rob Latin America of her resources while turning over a small rebate to a few members of a corrupt aristocracy, which in turn invests not in its own country for its own people's welfare but in the banks of Switzerland and the playgrounds of the world.

Here we see racism in its more sophisticated form: neo-colonialism. The Bible and the annals of history are replete with tragic stories of one brother robbing another of his birthright and thereby insuring generations of strife and enmity. We can hardly escape such a judgment in Latin America, any more than we have been able to escape the harvest of hate sown in Vietnam by a century of French exploitation.

There is the convenient temptation to attribute the current turmoil and bitterness throughout the world to the presence of a Communist conspiracy to undermine Europe and America, but the potential explosiveness of our world situation is much more attributable to disillusionment with the promises of Christianity and technology.

The revolutionary leaders of Africa, Asia and Latin America have virtually all received their education in the capitals of the West. Their earliest training often occurred in Christian missionary schools. Here their sense of dignity was established and they learned that all men were sons of God. In recent years their countries have been invaded by automobiles, Coca-Cola and Hollywood, so that even remote villages have become aware of the wonders and blessings available to God's white children.

Once the aspirations and appetites of the world have been whetted by the marvels of Western technology and the self-image of a people awakened by religion, one cannot hope to keep people locked out of the earthly kingdom of wealth, health and happiness. Either they share in the blessings of the world or they organize to break down and overthrow those structures or governments which stand in the way of their goals.

Former generations could not conceive of such luxury, but their children now take this vision and demand that it become a reality. And when they look around and see that the only people who do not share in the abundance of Western technology are colored people, it is an almost inescapable conclusion that their condition and their exploitation are somehow related to their color and the racism of the white Western world.

This is a treacherous foundation for a world house. Racism can well be that corrosive evil that will bring down the curtain on Western civilization. Arnold Toynbee has said that some twenty-six civilizations have risen upon the face of the earth. Almost all of them have descended into the junk heaps of destruction. The decline and fall of these civilizations, according to Toynbee, was not caused by external invasions but by internal decay. They failed to respond creatively to the challenges impinging upon them. If Western civilization does not now respond constructively to the challenge to banish racism, some future historian will have to say that a great civilization died because it lacked the soul and commitment to make justice a reality for all men.

Another grave problem that must be solved if we are to live creatively in our world house is that of poverty on an international scale. Like a monstrous octopus, it stretches its choking, prehensile tentacles into lands and villages all over the world. Two-thirds of the peoples of the world go to bed hungry at night. They are undernourished, ill-housed and shabbily clad. Many of them have no houses or beds to sleep in. Their only beds are the sidewalks of the cities and the dusty roads of the villages. Most of these poverty-stricken children of God have never seen a physician or a dentist.

There is nothing new about poverty. What is new, however, is that we now have the resources to get rid of it. Not too many years ago, Dr. Kirtley Mather, a Harvard geologist, wrote a book entitled *Enough and to Spare.*[2] He set forth the basic theme that famine is wholly unnecessary in the modern world. Today, therefore, the question on the agenda must read: why should there be hunger and privation in any land, in any city, at any table, when man has the resources and the scientific know-how to provide all mankind with the basic necessities of life? Even deserts can be irrigated and topsoil can be replaced. We cannot complain of a lack of land, for there are 25 million square miles of tillable land on earth, of which we are using less than seven million. We have amazing knowledge of vitamins, nutrition, the chemistry of food and the versatility of atoms. There is no deficit in human resources; the deficit is in human will.

This does not mean that we can overlook the enormous acceleration in the rate of growth of the world's population. The population explosion is very real, and it must be faced squarely if we are to avoid, in centuries ahead, a "standing room only" situation on these earthly shores. Most of the large undeveloped nations in the world today are confronted with the problem of excess population in relation to resources. But even this problem will be greatly diminished by wiping out poverty. When people see more opportunities for better education and greater economic security, they begin to consider whether a smaller family might not be better for themselves and for their children. In other words, I doubt that there can be a stabilization of the population without a prior stabilization of economic resources.

The time has come for an all-out world war against poverty. The rich nations must use their vast resources of wealth to develop the underdeveloped, school the unschooled and feed the unfed. The well-off and the secure have too often become indifferent and oblivious to the poverty and deprivation in their midst. The poor in our countries have been shut out of our minds, and driven from the mainstream of our societies, because we have allowed them to become invisible. Ultimately a great nation is a compassionate nation. No individual or nation can be great if it does not have a concern for "the least of these."

The first step in the worldwide war against poverty is passionate commitment. All the wealthy nations—America, Britain, Russia, Canada, Australia, and those of Western Europe—must see it as a moral obligation to provide capital and technical assistance to the underdeveloped areas. These rich nations have only scratched the surface in their commitment. There is need now for a general strategy of support. Sketchy aid here and there will not suffice, nor will it sustain economic growth. There must be a sustained effort extending through many years. The wealthy nations of the world must promptly initiate a massive, sustained Marshall Plan for

Asia, Africa and South America. If they would allocate just 2 percent of their gross national product annually for a period of ten or twenty years for the development of the under-developed nations, mankind would go a long way toward conquering the ancient enemy, poverty.

The aid program that I am suggesting must not be used by the wealthy nations as a surreptitious means to control the poor nations. Such an approach would lead to a new form of paternalism and a neocolonialism which no self-respecting nation could accept. Ultimately, foreign aid programs must be motivated by a compassionate and committed effort to wipe poverty, ignorance and disease from the face of the earth. Money devoid of genuine empathy is like salt devoid of savor, good for nothing except to be trodden under foot of men.

The West must enter into the program with humility and penitence and a sober realization that everything will not always "go our way." It cannot be forgotten that the Western powers were but yesterday the colonial masters. The house of the West is far from in order, and its hands are far from clean.

We must have patience. We must be willing to understand why many of the young nations will have to pass through the same extremism, revolution and aggression that formed our own history. Every new government confronts overwhelming problems. During the days when they were struggling to remove the yoke of colonialism, there was a kind of preexistent unity of purpose that kept things moving in one solid direction. But as soon as independence emerges, all the grim problems of life confront them with stark realism: the lack of capital, the strangulating poverty, the uncontrollable birth rates and, above all, the high aspirational level of their own people. The postcolonial period is more difficult and precarious than the colonial struggle itself.

The West must also understand that its economic growth took place under rather propitious circumstances. Most of the Western nations were relatively underpopulated when they surged forward economically, and they were greatly endowed with the iron ore and coal that were needed for launching industry. Most of the young governments of the world today have come into being without these advantages, and, above all, they confront staggering problems of over-population. There is no possible way for them to make it without aid and assistance.

A genuine program on the part of the wealthy nations to make prosperity a reality for the poor nations will in the final analysis enlarge the prosperity of all. One of the best proofs that reality hinges on moral foundations is the fact that when men and governments work devotedly for the good of others, they achieve their own enrichment in the process.

From time immemorial men have lived by the principle that "self-preservation is the first law of life." But this is a false assumption. I would say that other-preservation is the first law of life. It is the first law of life precisely because we cannot preserve self without being concerned about preserving other selves. The universe is so structured that things go awry if men are not diligent in their cultivation of the other-regarding dimension. "I" cannot reach fulfillment without "thou." The self cannot be self without other selves. Self-concern without other-concern is like a tributary that has no outward flow to the ocean. Stagnant, still and stale, it lacks both life and freshness. Nothing would be more disastrous and out of harmony with our self-interest than for the developed nations to travel a dead-end road of inordinate selfishness. We are in the fortunate position of having our deepest sense of morality coalesce with our self-interest.

But the real reason that we must use our resources to outlaw poverty goes beyond material concerns to the quality of our mind and spirit. Deeply woven into the fiber of our religious tradition is the conviction that men are made in the image of God, and that they are souls of infinite metaphysical value. If we accept this as a profound moral fact, we cannot be content to see men hungry, to see men victimized with ill-health, when we have the means to help them. In the final analysis, the rich must not ignore the poor because both rich and poor are tied together. They entered the same mysterious gateway of human birth, into the same adventure of mortal life.

All men are interdependent. Every nation is an heir of a vast treasury of ideas and labor to which both the living and the dead of all nations have contributed. Whether we realize it or not, each of us lives eternally "in the red." We are everlasting debtors to known and unknown men and women. When we arise in the morning, we go into the bathroom where we reach for a sponge which is provided for us by a Pacific Islander. We reach for soap that is created for us by a European. Then at the table we drink coffee which is provided for us by a South American, or tea by a Chinese or cocoa by a West African. Before we leave for our jobs we are already beholden to more than half of the world.

In a real sense, all life is interrelated. The agony of the poor impoverishes the rich; the betterment of the poor enriches the rich. We are inevitably our brother's keeper because we are our brother's brother. Whatever affects one directly affects all indirectly.

A final problem that mankind must solve in order to survive in the world house that we have inherited is finding an alternative to war and human destruction. Recent events have vividly reminded us that nations are not reducing but rather increasing their arsenals of weapons of mass destruction. The best brains in the highly developed nations of the world are devoted to military technology. The proliferation of nuclear weapons has not been halted, in spite of the limited-test-ban treaty.

In this day of man's highest technical achievement, in this day of dazzling discovery, of novel opportunities, loftier dignities and fuller freedoms for all, there is no excuse for the kind of blind craving for power and resources that provoked the wars of previous generations. There is no need to fight for food and land. Science has provided us with adequate means of survival and transportation, which make it possible to enjoy the fullness of this great earth. The question now is, do we have the morality and courage required to live together as brothers and not be afraid?

One of the most persistent ambiguities we face is that everybody talks about peace as a goal, but among the wielders of power peace is practically nobody's business. Many men cry "Peace! Peace!" but they refuse to do the things that make for peace.

The large power blocs talk passionately of pursuing peace while expanding defense budgets that already bulge, enlarging already awesome armies and devising ever more devastating weapons. Call the roll of those who sing the glad tidings of peace and one's ears will be surprised by the responding sounds. The heads of all the nations issue clarion calls for peace, yet they come to the peace table accompanied by bands of brigands each bearing unsheathed swords.

The stages of history are replete with the chants and choruses of the conquerors of old who came killing in pursuit of peace. Alexander, Genghis Khan, Julius Caesar, Charlemagne and Napoleon were akin in seeking a peaceful world order, a world fashioned after their selfish conceptions of an ideal existence. Each sought a world at peace which would personify his egotistic dreams. Even within the life span of most of us, another megalomaniac strode across the world stage. He sent his blitzkrieg-bent legions blazing across Europe, bringing havoc and holocaust in his wake. There is grave irony in the fact that Hitler could come forth, following nakedly aggressive expansionist theories, and do it all in the name of peace.

So when in this day I see the leaders of nations again talking peace while preparing for war, I take fearful pause. When I see our country today intervening in what is basically a civil war, mutilating hundreds of thousands of Vietnamese children with napalm, burning villages and rice fields at random, painting the valleys of that small Asian country red with human blood, leaving broken bodies in countless ditches and sending home half-men, mutilated mentally and physically; when I see the unwillingness of our government to create the atmosphere for a negotiated settlement of this awful conflict by halting bombings in the North and agreeing unequivocally to talk with the Vietcong—and all this in the name of pursuing the goal of peace—I tremble for our world. I do so not only from dire recall of the nightmares wreaked in the wars of yesterday, but also from dreadful realization of today's possible nuclear destructiveness and tomorrow's even more calamitous prospects.

Before it is too late, we must narrow the gaping chasm between our proclamations of peace and our lowly deeds which precipitate and perpetuate war. We are called upon to look up from the quagmire of military programs and defense commitments and read the warnings on history's signposts.

One day we must come to see that peace is not merely

a distant goal that we seek but a means by which we arrive at that goal. We must pursue peaceful ends through peaceful means. How much longer must we play at deadly war games before we heed the plaintive pleas of the unnumbered dead and maimed of past wars?

President John F. Kennedy said on one occasion, "Mankind must put an end to war or war will put an end to mankind." Wisdom born of experience should tell us that war is obsolete. There may have been a time when war served as a negative good by preventing the spread and growth of an evil force, but the destructive power of modern weapons eliminates even the possibility that war may serve any good at all. If we assume that life is worth living and that man has a right to survive, then we must find an alternative to war. In a day when vehicles hurtle through outer space and guided ballistic missiles carve highways of death through the stratosphere, no nation can claim victory in war. A so-called limited war will leave little more than a calamitous legacy of human suffering, political turmoil and spiritual disillusionment. A world war will leave only smoldering ashes as mute testimony of a human race whose folly led inexorably to ultimate death. If modern man continues to flirt unhesitatingly with war, he will transform his earthly habitat into an inferno such as even the mind of Dante could not imagine.

Therefore I suggest that the philosophy and strategy of nonviolence become immediately a subject for study and for serious experimentation in every field of human conflict, by no means excluding the relations between nations. It is, after all, nation-states which make war, which have produced the weapons that threaten the survival of mankind and which are both genocidal and suicidal in character.

We have ancient habits to deal with, vast structures of power, indescribably complicated problems to solve. But unless we abdicate our humanity altogether and succumb to fear and impotence in the presence of the weapons we have ourselves created, it is as possible and as urgent to put an end to war and violence between nations as it is to put an end to poverty and racial injustice.

The United Nations is a gesture in the direction of nonviolence on a world scale. There, at least, states that oppose one another have sought to do so with words instead of with weapons. But true nonviolence is more than the absence of violence. It is the persistent and determined application of peaceable power to offenses against the community—in this case the world community. As the United Nations moves ahead with the giant tasks confronting it, I would hope that it would earnestly examine the uses of nonviolent direct action.

I do not minimize the complexity of the problems that need to be faced in achieving disarmament and peace. But I am convinced that we shall not have the will, the courage and the insight to deal with such matters unless in this field we are prepared to undergo a mental and spiritual re-evaluation, a change of focus which will enable us to see that the things that seem most real and powerful are indeed now unreal and have come under sentence of death. We need to make a supreme effort to generate the readiness, indeed the eagerness, to enter into the new world which is now possible, "the city which hath foundation, whose Building and Maker is God."

It is not enough to say, "We must not wage war." It is necessary to love peace and sacrifice for it. We must concentrate not merely on the eradication of war but on the affirmation of peace. A fascinating story about Ulysses and the Sirens is preserved for us in Greek literature. The Sirens had the ability to sing so sweetly that sailors could not resist steering toward their island. Many ships were lured upon the rocks, and men forgot home, duty and honor as they flung themselves into the sea to be embraced by arms that drew them down to death. Ulysses, determined not to succumb to the Sirens, first decided to tie himself tightly to the mast of his boat and his crew stuffed their ears with wax. But finally he and his crew learned a better way to save themselves: they took on board the beautiful singer Orpheus, whose melodies were sweeter than the music of the Sirens. When Orpheus sang, who would bother to listen to the Sirens?

So we must see that peace represents a sweeter music, a cosmic melody that is far superior to the discords of war. Somehow we must transform the dynamics of the world power struggle from the nuclear arms race, which no one can win, to a creative contest to harness man's genius for the purpose of making peace and prosperity a reality for all the nations of the world. In short, we must shift the arms race into a "peace race." If we have the will and determination to mount such a peace offensive, we will unlock hitherto tightly sealed doors of hope and bring new light into the dark chambers of pessimism.

III

The stability of the large world house which is ours will involve a revolution of values to accompany the scientific and freedom revolutions engulfing the earth. We must rapidly begin the shift from a "thing"-oriented society to a "person"-oriented society. When machines and computers, profit motives and property rights are considered more important than people, the giant triplets of racism, materialism and militarism are incapable of being conquered. A civilization can flounder as readily in the face of moral and spiritual bankruptcy as it can through financial bankruptcy.

This revolution of values must go beyond traditional capitalism and Communism. We must honestly admit that capitalism has often left a gulf between superfluous wealth and abject poverty, has created conditions permitting necessities to be taken from the many to give luxuries to the few, and has encourage smallhearted men to become cold and conscienceless so that, like Dives before Lazarus, they are unmoved by suffering, poverty-stricken humanity. The profit motive, when it is the sole basis of an economic system, encourages a cutthroat competition and selfish ambition that inspire men to be more I-centered than thou-centered. Equally, Communism reduces men to a cog in the wheel of the state. The Communist may object, saying that in Marxian theory the state is an "interim reality" that will "wither away" when the classless society emerges. True—in theory; but it is also true that, while the state lasts, it is an end in itself. Man is a means to that end. He has no inalienable rights. His only rights are derived from, and conferred by, the state. Under such a system the fountain of freedom runs dry. Restricted are man's liberties of press and assembly, his freedom to vote and his freedom to listen and to read.

Truth is found neither in traditional capitalism nor in classical Communism. Each represents a partial truth. Capitalism fails to see the truth in collectivism. Communism fails to see the truth in individualism. Capitalism fails to realize that life is social. Communism fails to realize that life is personal. The good and just society is neither the thesis of capitalism nor the antithesis of Communism, but a socially conscious democracy which reconciles the truths of individualism and collectivism.

We have seen some moves in this direction. The Soviet Union has gradually moved away from its rigid Communism and begun to concern itself with consumer products, art and a general increase in benefits to the individual citizen. At the same time, through constant social reforms, we have seen many modifications in laissez-faire capitalism. The problems we now face must take us beyond slogans for their solution. In the final analysis, the right-wing slogans on "government control" and "creeping socialism" are as meaningless and adolescent as the Chinese Red Guard slogans against "bourgeois revisionism." An intelligent approach to the problems of poverty and racism will cause us to see that the words of the Psalmist—"The earth is the Lord's and the fullness thereof"—are still a judgment upon our use and abuse of the wealth and resources with which we have been endowed.

A true revolution of value will soon cause us to question the fairness and justice of many of our past and present policies. We are called to play the Good Samaritan on life's roadside; but that will be only an initial act. One day the whole Jericho Road must be transformed so that men and women will not be beaten and robbed as they make their journey through life. True compassion is more than flinging a coin to a beggar; it understands that an edifice which produces beggars needs restructuring.

A true revolution of values will soon look uneasily on the glaring contrast of poverty and wealth. With righteous indignation, it will look at thousands of working people displaced from their jobs with reduced incomes as a result of automation while the profits of the employers remain intact, and say: "This is not just." It will look across the oceans and see individual capitalists of the West investing huge sums of money in Asia, Africa and South America, only to take the profits out with no concern for the social betterment of the countries, and say: "This is not just." It will look at our alliance with the landed gentry of Latin America and say: "This is not just." The Western arrogance of feeling that it has everything to teach others and nothing to learn from them is not just. A true revolution of values will lay hands on the world order and say of war: "This way of settling differences is not just." This business of burning human beings with napalm, of filling our nation's homes with orphans and widows, of injecting poisonous drugs of hate into the veins of peoples normally humane, of sending men home from dark and bloody battlefields physically handicapped and psychologically deranged cannot be reconciled with wisdom, justice and love. A nation that continues year after year to spend more money on military defense than on programs of social uplift is approaching spiritual death.

America, the richest and most powerful nation in the world, can well lead the way in this revolution of values. There is nothing to prevent us from paying adequate wages to schoolteachers, social workers and other servants of the public to insure that we have the best available personnel in these positions which are charged with the responsibility of guiding our future generations. There is nothing but a lack of social vision to prevent us from paying an adequate wage to every American citizen whether he be a hospital worker, laundry worker, maid or day laborer. There is nothing except shortsightedness to prevent us from guaranteeing an annual minimum—and *livable*—income for every American family. There is nothing, except a tragic death wish, to prevent us from reordering our priorities, so that the pursuit of peace will take precedence over the pursuit of war. There is nothing to keep us from remolding a recalcitrant status quo with bruised hands until we have fashioned it into a brotherhood.

This kind of positive revolution of values is our best defense against Communism. War is not the answer. Communism will never be defeated by the use of atomic bombs or nuclear weapons. Let us not join those who shout war and who through their misguided passions urge the United States to relinquish its participation in the United Nations. These are days which demand wise restraint and calm reasonableness. We must not call everyone a Communist or an appeaser who advocates the seating of Red China in the United Nations, or who recognizes that hate and hysteria are not the final answers to the problems of these turbulent days. We must not engage in a negative anti-Communism, but rather in a positive thrust for democracy, realizing that our greatest defense against Communism is to take offensive action in behalf of justice. We must with affirmative action seek to remove those conditions of poverty, insecurity and injustice which are the fertile soil in which the seed of Communism grows and develops.

These are revolutionary times. All over the globe men are revolting against old systems of exploitation and oppression, and out of the wombs of a frail world new systems of justice and equality are being born. The shirtless and barefoot people of the earth are rising up as never before. "The people who sat in darkness have seen a great light." We in the West must support these revolutions. It is a sad fact that, because of comfort, complacency, a morbid fear of Communism and our proneness to adjust to injustice, the Western nations that initiated so much of the revolutionary spirit of the modern world have now become the arch antirevolutionaries. This has driven many to feel that only Marxism has the revolutionary spirit. Communism is a judgment on our failure to make democracy real and to follow through on the revolutions that we initiated. Our only hope today lies in our ability to recapture the revolutionary spirit and go out into a sometimes hostile world declaring eternal opposition to poverty, racism and militarism. With this powerful commitment we shall boldly challenge the status quo and unjust mores and thereby speed the day when "every valley shall be exalted, and every mountain and hill shall be made low: and the crooked shall be made straight and the rough places plain."

A genuine revolution of values means in the final analysis that our loyalties must become ecumenical rather than sectional. Every nation must now develop an overriding loyalty to mankind as a whole in order to preserve the best in their individual societies.

This call for a worldwide fellowship that lifts neighborly concern beyond one's tribe, race, class and nation is in reality a call for an all-embracing and unconditional love for all men. This often misunderstood and misinterpreted concept has now become an absolute necessity for the survival of man. When I speak of love, I am speaking of that force which all the great religions have seen as the supreme unifying principle of life. Love is the key that unlocks the door which leads to ultimate reality. This Hindu-Muslim-Christian-Jewish-Buddhist belief about ultimate reality is beautifully summed up in the First Epistle of Saint John:

Let us love one another: for love is of God:
and every one that loveth is born of God, and
knoweth God. He that loveth not knoweth not
God; for God is love. . . . If we love one another,
God dwelleth in us, and his love is perfected in us.

Let us hope that this spirit will become the order of the day. We can no longer afford to worship the God of hate or bow before the altar of retaliation. The oceans of history are made turbulent by the ever-rising tides of hate. History is cluttered with the wreckage of nations and individuals who pursued this self-defeating path of hate. As Arnold Toynbee once said in a speech: "Love is the ultimate force that makes for the saving choice of life and good against the damning choice of death and evil. Therefore the first hope in our inventory must be the hope that love is going to have the last word."

We are now faced with the fact that tomorrow is today. We are confronted with the fierce urgency of *now*. In this unfolding conundrum of life and history there is such a thing as being too late. Procrastination is still the thief of time. Life often leaves us standing bare, naked and dejected with a lost opportunity. The "tide in the affairs of men" does not remain at the flood; it ebbs. We may cry out desperately for time to pause in her passage, but time is deaf to every plea and rushes on. Over the bleached bones and jumbled residues of numerous civilizations are written the pathetic words: "Too late." There is an invisible book of life that faithfully records our vigilance or our neglect. "The moving finger writes, and having writ moves on. . . ." We still have a choice today: nonviolent coexistence or violent coannihilation. This may well be mankind's last chance to choose between chaos and community.

APPENDIX

Programs and Prospects

EDUCATION

American society has emphasized education more than European society. The purpose is to use education to make a break between the occupation of the parents and those of their children. The schools have been the historic routes of social mobility. But when Negroes and others of the underclass now ask that schools play the same function for them, many within and outside the school system answer that the schools cannot do the job. They would impose on the family the whole task of preparing and leading youngsters into educational advance. And this reluctance to engage with the great issue of our day—the full emancipation and equality of Negroes and the poor—comes at a time when education is more than ever the passport to decent economic positions.

Whatever pathology may exist in Negro families is far exceeded by this social pathology in the school system that refuses to accept a responsibility that no one else can bear and then scapegoats Negro families for failing to do the job. The scattered evidence suggesting that family life is important in educational progress provides only partial support for the rationalizations of educators; for family life explains only a small portion of learning difficulties. The job of the school is to teach so well that family background is no longer an issue.

The sad truth is that American schools, by and large, do not know how to teach—nor frequently what to teach. The ineffectiveness in teaching reading skills to many young people, whether white or black, poor or rich, strongly indicts foundations and government for not spending funds effectively to find out what different kinds of reading experiences are needed by youth with various learning styles at various points in their life. While we aim for the moon, we putter around in academic gardens without even a relief map.

We have been timid in trying to improve schools. Operation Headstart has shown that a little work before school cannot insulate children from the impact of poor teaching and poor schools. Programs that throw a little money into a school for counseling or remedial reading instruction cannot prepare youth for the educational needs of today.

The task is considerable; it is not merely to bring Negroes up to higher educational levels, but to close the gap between their educational levels and those of whites. If this does not happen, as Negroes advance educationally, whites will be moving ahead even more rapidly.

Despite the despair and regret over past educational failures, we have not seriously begun to approach the needs of Negro and poor youngsters. The data of a Carnegie-sponsored study show that the differences in educational expenditures between center cities and suburbs have widened since the late fifties. Instead of spending relatively more on the disadvantaged of the big cities, we are spending less— another tragic example of the inversion of priorities which plagues American society.

Much more money has to be spent on education of the children of the poor; the rate of increase in expenditures for the poor has to be much greater than for the well-off if the children of the poor are to catch up.

The road to effective education requires helping teachers to teach more effectively. The use of nonprofessional aides would reduce class size and provide needed assistance to teachers. More direct training and aid in teaching young-sters from low-income families is needed. Parents should be involved in the schools to a much greater extent, breaking down the barriers between professionals and the community that they serve. Education is too important today to be left to professional fads and needs. This is not to assert that profes-sional competence is unnecessary, but that there must be a greater evidence of competence and a new and creative link between parents and schools.

Schools have to be infused with a mission if they are to be successful. The mission is clear: the rapid improvement of the school performance of Negroes and other poor children. If this does not happen, America will suffer for decades to come. Where a missionary zeal has been demonstrated by school administrators and teachers, and where this dedica-tion has been backed by competence, funds and a desire to involve parents, much has been accomplished. But by and large American educators, despite occasional rhetoric to the contrary, have not dedicated themselves to the rapid im-provement of the education of the poor.

Aside from finances, a major reason for the absence of dedication to the great problem of contemporary Ameri-can education has been the issue of integration. Integrated education has been charged with diminishing the qual-ity education of whites. Recent studies by James Coleman

206 | MARTIN LUTHER KING, JR.

for the U.S. Office of Education dispute this. Integrated education *does not* retard white students while it *does* improve the performance of Negro.

Quality education for all is most likely to come through educational parks which bring together in one place all the students of a large area. Because of the economies of large-scale operation, the educational park will make practical a multiplicity of teaching specialists and superb facilities. Involving students from a wide area attracted by the superior opportunities, such a plan will guarantee school integration even before housing is desegregated.

The educational park is likely to be the next great structure for education. Funds should come from the federal government, which must move from supporting the fringes of education to supporting the basics—the teachers and the facilities with which they work. The federal government should begin to provide building grants to local school districts and groups of districts so that educational parks can be constructed. Building grants should go to localities—cities and suburbs—which locate schools so as to promote integration. The arbitrary lines of government should not serve to balkanize America into white and black schools and communities.

The location of new school buildings affects the long-term prospects of education. In the short run, schools in ghetto areas must be improved. Authentic efforts to upgrade them must be pursued. But the drive for immediate improvements in segregated schools should not retard progress toward integrated education later. New schools should be planned so as to fit into some aspect of an educational park. Even during this period, while metropolitan districts are being remade by change and growth, partial integration can occur if neighborhood schools participate during part of the school day in joint and meaningful activities. Max Wolff, the father of the educational park idea, has suggested ways of using existing buildings and temporary structures to produce some of the effects of the educational park.

The United States is far from providing each child with as much education as he can use. Our school system still primarily functions as a system of exclusion. For the oldest generation of Negroes the time for effective educational remedies is probably already past; but there is an enormous reservoir of talent among Negro and other poor youth. This society has to develop that talent. The unrealized capacities of many of our youth are an indictment of our society's lack of concern for justice and its proclivity for wasting human resources. As with so much else in this potentially great society, injustice and waste go together and endanger stability.

EMPLOYMENT

Economic expansion cannot alone do the job of improving the employment situation of Negroes. It provides the base for improvement but other things must be constructed upon it, especially if the tragic situation of youth is to be solved. In a booming economy Negro youth are afflicted with unemployment as though in an economic crisis. They are the explosive outsiders of the American expansion.

The insistence on educational certificates and credentials for skilled and semiskilled jobs is keeping Negroes out of both the private business sector and government employment. Negro exclusion is not the purpose of the insistence upon credentials, but it is its inevitable consequence today. The orientation of personnel offices should be "Jobs First, Training Later." Unfortunately, the job policy of the federal programs has largely been the reverse, with the result that people are being trained for nonexistent jobs.

"Training" becomes a way of avoiding the issue of employment, for it does not ask the employer to change his policies and job structures. Instead of training for uncertain jobs, the policy of the government should be to subsidize American business to employ individuals whose education is limited. This policy may be considered a bribe by some, but it is a step consonant with reality. We require a vast expansion of present programs of on-the-job training in which training costs are absorbed by the government; at another level, employers could be granted reduced taxes if they employed difficult-to-place workers. (Many states have "merit" reductions in unemployment taxes for employers with a good record of sustained employment; why not a "merit" reward for hiring the difficult-to-place? In some European countries employers are required to have a certain percentage of physically handicapped persons in their labor force; why not a similar requirement here for the difficult-to-place?)

The big, new, attractive thrust of Negro employment is in the nonprofessional services. A high percentage of these jobs is in public employment. The human services—medical attention, social services, neighborhood amenities of various kinds—are in scarce supply in this country, especially in localities of poverty. The traditional way of providing manpower for these jobs—degree-granting programs—cannot fill all the niches that are opening up. The traditional job requirements are a barrier to attaining an adequate supply of personnel, especially if the number of jobs expands to meet the existing need.

The expansion of the human services can be the missing industry that will soak up the unemployment that persists in the United States. Secretary of Labor W. Willard Wirtz has talked about the missing industry that would change the employment scene in America. The expansion of human services is that industry—it is labor

intensive, requiring manpower immediately rather than heavy capi-
tal investment as in construction or other fields; it fills a great need
not met by private enterprise; it involves labor that can be trained
and developed on the job.

The growth of the human services should be rapid. It
should be developed in a manner ensuring that *the jobs gener-*
ated will not primarily be for professionals with college and postgradu-
ate diplomas but for people from the neighborhoods who can perform
important functions for their neighbors. As with private enterprise, rigid credentials have monopolized the entry routes
into human services employment. But, as Frank Riessman
and Arthur Pearl have argued in their book, *New Careers for*
the Poor, less educated people can do many of the tasks now
performed by the highly educated as well as many other new
and necessary tasks.

Universities adapting to the new needs of the day must
learn how to develop the abilities of people who have had
trouble with school in their youth and have not earned their
credentials. They should be trained on the job, get university credit for their experience, learn in relevant courses and
develop a liberal-arts knowledge that is built around their
concerns. We need what S. M. Miller has called "second-
chance universities." A democratic educational system requires multiple doors.

The Freedom Budget of A. P. Randolph is important because it provides a basis for common action with labor and
other groups in utilizing the economic growth of this nation
to benefit the poor as well as the rich. It raises the possibility
of rebuilding America so that private affluence is not accompanied by public squalor of slums and distress.

The Freedom Budget, the expansion of private employment and nonprofessional opportunities cannot, however,
provide full employment for Negroes. Many youths are not

listed as unemployed because in despair they have left the labor market completely. They are psychologically disabled and cannot be rescued by conventional employment. They need special workplaces where their irregularity as workers can be accepted until they have restored their habits of discipline. The jobs should nevertheless be jobs and understood as such, not given the false label of "training."

Among the employed, where discrimination continues to operate, discrepancies in pay between Negroes and whites are ubiquitous. This discrepancy occurs because (1) Negroes are paid less for the same job; (2) a heavier proportion of Negroes work in the low-wage South; and (3) a smaller percentage of Negroes are in high-wage jobs. The first could be eliminated by more effective policing of fair employment practices. The second is partly changing as Negroes leave the South, though more important would be effective unionization of Southern plants. The third requires strong effort of government and private employers and schools and colleges to develop upgrading practices which give Negroes a chance at the better jobs.

RIGHTS

The proliferating bureaucracies in a complex industrial society tend to curtail democratic rights. Those that affect the affluent and powerful can be handled by appeals to the courts, which have power to prohibit unwarranted decrees or decisions beyond the scope of proper authority. The poor, however, are helpless. In welfare, public housing and education, arbitrary abuse of power cannot be arrested by means readily available to the victimized. In most cases the victim does not know he has legal redress and accepts the role of a supplicant unprotected by rules, regulations and safeguards. In some cases, the issue is uncontrolled bureaucratic or political power; in others, the question is the relationship between professionals and those they have a duty to service but too often humiliate or neglect.

Slowly, however, the concept is emerging that beneficiaries of welfare measures are not beggars but citizens endowed with rights defined by law. The principle that citizens should have "maximum feasible participation" in community planning and other decisions affecting their lives is growing. The rights of all parents—not only the wealthy—to have a significant role in educational decisions affecting their children is still another developing concept. From a variety of different directions, the strands are drawing together for a contemporary social and economic Bill of Rights to supplement the Constitution's political Bill of Rights.

The new forms of rights are new methods of participation in decision-making. The concept of democracy is being pushed to deeper levels of meaning—from formal exercise of voting, still an issue in much of the United States for many Negroes, to effective participation in major decisions.

Two areas where the enlargement of rights has taken significant organized form are welfare unions and tenant unions. The untold story of bureaucratic abuse of welfare recipients is heartrending. The humiliation imposed is bad enough, but worse is the fact that recipients are denied substantial benefits granted to them by the law. Cloward has estimated that welfare clients actually receive only 50 percent of the benefits the law provides because they are consciously kept ignorant of their rights. As individuals they have no means of informing themselves or of asserting their right to withheld benefits. Through welfare unions, however, the maximum legal limit can be obtained and deeper solutions to the problems of poverty can be sought with organized strength and collective judgment.

Tenant unions are one answer to abuses resulting from the growth of public housing, which has made some cities the largest landlords and the largest bureaucracies in the land. Our experience in Chicago indicates that tenant unions can not only be built but can achieve sophisticated ends such as formal written and detailed collective agreements with both private and public landlords.

Welfare and tenant unions need legislation to protect members from reprisals and intimidation. Fear of loss of welfare or eviction from apartments inhibits organization. Just as labor obtained the right to organize expressed in the Wagner Act, welfare recipients and tenants need the same legal shield to facilitate mass organization.

HOUSING

The American housing industry is a disgrace to a society which can confidently plan to get to the moon. The costs of construction have risen more rapidly than most other items. Technological advances in housing construction are regularly heralded and seldom implemented. The employment situation is a scandal—it tends to be a lily-white industry with as many intricate steps to entrance as the *Social Register*. Banks and government policy have actively encouraged and even required segregated housing; federal mortgage policy has only recently changed to favor some integrated housing.

The end result is that the United States is today a more segregated country in many respects than it was twenty years ago. Problems of education, transportation to jobs and decent living conditions are all made difficult because housing is so rigidly segregated. The expansion of suburbia and migration from the South have worsened big-city segregation. The suburbs are white nooses around the black necks of the cities. Housing deteriorates in central cities; urban renewal has been Negro removal and has benefited big merchants and real estate interests; and suburbs expand with little regard for what happens to the rest of America.

Both rehabilitation and some new building in predominantly Negro areas is immediately needed to alleviate inhuman conditions. But this should be done without foreclosing possibilities of later integration.

With the prospect of a new building boom in the United States and the emergence of new towns or communities, we must insure the development of integrated housing. The new and rehabilitated housing in ghetto areas should be temporary: constructed for a relatively short-term period of fifteen to twenty years. Units should be built with a plan to tear them down at the end of that period as housing integration is advanced. The financing and taxing of the housing should reflect this relatively short-term use; depreciation should be for a twenty-year period, rather than for the conventional fifty years, and demolition should be required when depreciation terminates. The construction activities should be subsidized through expansion of present-day housing subsidies, tax write-offs, low-cost rehabilitation loans and the like.

The interim solutions for ghetto housing should not obscure the need for strict enforcement of sound housing practices. But inspection, fair housing, even rehabilitation cannot solve the problems of housing for the segregated poor. New, good housing available at low cost is needed to satisfy the dwelling needs of the underclass. While housing expenditures are a fourth or a fifth of a family's expenditures, they are less than a twentieth of governmental expenditures. Once more priorities have to be reversed; the federal government subsidizes the nonpoor twice as much as the poor when we include various forms of subsidies such as middle-income public housing, tax deductions for mortgage interest and real estate taxes. The federal government should be subsidizing housing activities on such a scale that all American housing meets at least minimal standards of adequacy.

Housing is too important to be left to private enterprise with only minor government effort to shape policy. We need the equivalent of a Medicare for housing.

The possibilities for decent, integrated housing are not as remote as increasing segregation in large cities would indicate. The model cities and new towns concepts suggest ways to remake cities and their surrounding areas. The United States is now a metropolitan nation and will become more so. Government policy can powerfully facilitate an integrated society by refusing to subsidize planned segregation (which took place under government subsidies to suburban home-owners in the fifties and sixties) and by requiring integrated communities.

While we cannot resolve the issues of decent, integrated housing immediately, we are now making the choices which will determine whether we can achieve these goals in forth-coming decades. We cannot afford to make these choices poorly.

NOTES

CHAPTER I. WHERE ARE WE?

1. Article I, section 2, paragraph 3.
2. *Vital Statistics, 1961,* New York City Department of Health.
3. *New York Times,* February 14, 1967.
4. 1960 Census.
5. Ibid.
6. *Newsweek* Survey–Harris Poll, August 22, 1966.
7. Southern Regional Council, 1966.
8. Donald R. Matthews and James W. Prothro, *Negroes and the New Southern Politics,* Harcourt, Brace and World, 1966, p. 148.

CHAPTER II. BLACK POWER

1. Southern Regional Council, 1966.
2. Harper, 1964, pp. 162ff.
3. Knopf, 1956.
4. In *The Negro Protest,* Kenneth B. Clark (ed.), Beacon, 1963.
5. Evergreen, 1966.
6. *The Fire Next Time,* Dial, 1963, pp. 22–23.
7. November 1966.
8. Op. cit., p. 255.

CHAPTER III.
RACISM AND THE WHITE BACKLASH

1. Eriksson, 1966, p. 1.

2. Scribner's, 1965, p. 9.

3. Rev. ed., Viking, 1947, p. 98.

4. *Douglass Monthly,* January, 1863.

5. Harper, 1944, pp. 1021–1022.

6. Fall 1966.

7. For an elaboration of this theory, see *Why We Can't Wait,* Harper, 1964, pp. 146–153.

CHAPTER IV.
THE DILEMMA OF NEGRO AMERICANS

1. *The Complete Poems of Paul Laurence Dunbar,* Dodd, Mead, 1950, p. 9.

2. Beacon, 1955.

3. Harcourt, Brace, 1940, pp. 130–131.

4. *The Dream Keeper,* Knopf, 1954, p. 73.

CHAPTER V. WHERE WE ARE GOING

1. Scribner's, p. 254.

2. *Newsweek* Survey–Harris Poll, July 29, 1963, and August 22, 1966.

3. Op. cit., p. 481.

4. *The Progressive,* December 1966.

CHAPTER VI. THE WORLD HOUSE

1. Abraham Mitrie Rihbany, *Wise Men from the East and from the West,* Houghton Mifflin, 1922, p. 137.

2. Harper, 1944.

INDEX

Aaron, Henry, 135
Acton, Lord, 68
Adams, Herbert Baxter, 78
Adams, John Quincy, 80
adult delinquency, 114
AFL-CIO, 150, 151
Albany movement (1962), 36
Alfred the Great, 61
Ali, Muhammad, 135
altruism, 107
American Dilemma, An, 89–90
American Historical Association, 78
American Indians, 85, 141
Anderson, Marian, 134–135
Angola, 58
anti-Communism, 200
anti-Semitism, 65, 97–98
Appalachians, 141
Arnall, Ellis, 161
Ashe, Arthur, 135
Atlanta, Georgia, 153
Attucks, Crispus, 42

"Back to Africa" movement, 48
Baldwin, James, 54, 62–63, 135

Batista, Fulgencio, 60
Beacon Press, ix
Beard, Charles A., 75
Belafonte, Harry, 135
Benedict, Ruth, 73
Bill of Rights for the Disadvantaged, 143
Birmingham, Ala., 5, 18, 36, 52, 151–152, 166
Black Muslimism, 133
Black Power, xiv, xx, 3, 12, 18, 29ff., 61, 66, 72, 125
black supremacy, 133
Bookbinder, Hyman, 6
Brown, James, 135
Buckmaster, Henrietta, 112
Bull, Ole, 128
Bunche, Ralph J., 125, 135
bureaucracies, 210, 212
Burke, Edmund, 94
bus boycott, 59
business, Negro, 147–154

Calhoun, John, 80
Campanella, Roy, 135
capitalism, xi, 197

Capone, Al, 125
Carmichael, Stokely, 24–25, 27,
    28–29, 30, 31, 32–34, 56
Carnegie Quarterly, 90
Carver, George Washington, 43,
    135
Castro, Fidel, 60
Chamberlain, Wilt, 135
Charles, Ray, 135
Chicago, xvii, 121–124, 153–154
Chicago movements, xii–xiii, 2,
    46, 60, 96
Chicago Urban League, 123
church, *see* religion
Cicero, 55
Cicero, Ill., 125
CIO, 149
Civil Rights Act (1964), 85, 127
civil rights bill (1868), 85
civil rights movement, 2–3
Civil War, 82
Clark, Jim, 15
Clark, Kenneth, 117
Cloward, Richard L., 211
Coleman, James, 205–206
*Collections on the Natural History
    of the Caucasian and Negro
    Races,* 78
colonialism, 180
"color shock," 116–121
Columbia University, 78
Communism, 184, 196–197, 200
Conant, James B., 141
Congress on Racial Equality,
    see CORE
Connor, Bull, 15
Conrad, Earl, 71–72
Constitution (U.S.), xvi, 6, 138,
    211
consumer goods, 123, 172

CORE, 24, 25–27, 32
Cornell University, 78
Cullen, Countee, 135
culture, 9

Dante, 194
Davis, Ossie, 42
Davis, Sammy, Jr., 135
Deacons for Defense, 27
Declaration of Independence, 75
delinquency, 114
democracy, 11
Democratic Party, 158
Demonstration Cities, 86, 93
desegregation, 106
    see also integration,
        school desegregation,
        and segregation
disenfranchisement, 15
"Dixie," 43
Dixiecrats, 155
Dominican Republic, 141
Douglass, Frederick, 82–83, 84
Dred Scott decision, 79
Drew, Charles, 43
Du Bois, W. E. B., 118, 135
Dunbar, Paul Laurence, 110, 135
Dusk of Dawn, 118

economic inequality, 17
economics, 146–147
Edison, Thomas A., 178
education, 6, 7, 44–51, 163–164,
    170, 171, 185–186, 207
educational parks, 206
Eichmann, Adolf, 91
Einstein, Albert, 178
Ellington, Duke, 135
Ellison, Ralph, 135
Emancipation Proclamation, 83

empathy, 107

employment, 7, 10, 113, 153–154, 172, 207–210

see also labor *and* unemployment

Englewood (Chicago), 124

equality, 8

family problems, 110ff., 138, 170, 171, 203–204

Fanon, Frantz, 56, 67–68

Fauntroy, Walter, 100

Fifteenth Amendment, 85

Flowers, Richmond, 161

Fosdick, Harry Emerson, 105

Franklin, Benjamin, 75

Frazier, E. Franklin, 113

Freedom Budget, 39, 209

Freedom March (Miss.), xiii, 23–25, 100

"Freedom Now," 30, 32

Freedom Rides (1961), 36, 59

Freeman, Edward A., 78

Galbraith, John Kenneth, 174

Gandhi, Mahatma, 45

Garrison, William Lloyd, 82

Garvey, Marcus, 48

genocide, 74

George, Henry, 172–173

George III of England, 181

Ghana, 58

ghettos, 10, 19, 35, 36–37, 97–98, 107, 109, 118–123, 126–127, 153–155, 165, 169, 213

Gibson, Althea, 135

Gobineau, Arthur de (Count), 78

Goldwater, Barry, 155

Great Society, 93

Greeley, Horace, 82

Greenwood, Miss., 29

group unity, 131–132, 133

guaranteed income, xvi, 171, 173–174

Hamer, Fanny Lou, xviii–xix

Harvard University, 78

Hayes, Roland, 134

Henry, Patrick, 80

Hitler, Adolf, 65, 74

housing, 6, 35, 60, 123–127, 170–173, 212–214

see also ghettos

Hughes, Langston, 128, 135

Hugo, Victor, 179

ideology, 146

indentured servants, 76

Indians, American, 85, 141

Inequality of the Human Races, The, 78

infant mortality, 7

integrated housing, *see* housing

integration, 63 64, 213

see also desegregation, school desegregation, *and* segregation

intermarriage, 91

Invention of the Negro, The, 71

Irving, Washington, 180

Jackson, Jimmy Lee, 34

Jackson, Mahalia, 135

Jefferson, Thomas, 75, 80–81

Jesus, 88

Jews, 163–164

John Birch Society, 93

Johns Hopkins University, 78

Johnson, Jack, 135

Johnson, James Weldon, 135

Johnson, Lyndon B., x, xv,

1–2, 3–4, 34, 58, 93, 143
juvenile delinquency, 114

Kant, Immanuel, 103
Kelsey, George, 73
Kennedy, John F., 18, 157
Killens, John, 63
Ku Klux Klan, 93

labor, 7–8, 148–151, 159
    see also employment *and*
    unemployment
Lawndale (Chicago), 121–123
Lawson, James (Rev.), 25
Lehman, Herbert, 157
Lewis, Oscar, 97
Lincoln, Abraham, 80, 82–83, 155
living standards, 7, 13
Locke, John, 74
Longfellow, Henry Wadsworth, 68
Louis, Joe, 135
Lowndes County (Ala.), 50
lunch counters, 59

Maddox, Lester, 161
manhood, 39–42, 44, 99, 105–106, 133
    see also selfhood
March on Washington, 59
Marengo, Battle of, 128
marriage, 111, 113
Marxism, 197
masculinity, see manhood
materialism, 196
Mather, Cotton, 77
matriarchy, 113

Matthews, Donald R., 160
Matzeliger, Jan, 43
Mays, Willie, 135
McKay, Claude, 135
McKissick, Floyd, 24, 29, 30, 31–32, 56
Meredith, James, 23–25
Meredith Mississippi March,
    see Freedom March (Miss.)
Mexican Americans, 141
middle class, Negro, xvii, 127, 140–141
militarism, 197
Miller, S. M., 209
Milton, John, 101
Mississippi Freedom March, see
    Freedom March (Miss.)
Montgomery, Ala., 1, 9, 18, 45, 59
Moore, Bishop, 100
Moral Man and Immoral Society, 151
Morton, Samuel G., 78
"Mother to Son," 128
Myrdal, Gunnar, 89–90

National Liberation Front, 56
Negro Digest, 63
New Careers for the Poor, 209
New York school boycott, 159
Newcombe, Don, 135
newspapers, Negro, 132
Niebuhr, Reinhold, 151
Nietzsche, Friedrich W., 37
Nigeria, 58
nonviolent action, 17, 18, 20–21, 23ff., 59ff., 96, 137–139, 145–147, 195, 202
Notes on Virginia, 81–82
Nott, Josiah C., 74

Obama, Barack, xiv, xvii
open housing, *see* housing
Operation Breadbasket, 152–154
Operation Headstart, 204
organization for civil rights, 139,
    159–165
Orpheus, 196
Owens, Jesse, 137

Paine, Thomas, xiii, xviii, 75
Pearl, Arthur, 209
Peculiar Institution, The, 39
Pettigrew, Thomas, 97, 111
Plato, 81, 82
Poitier, Sidney, 135
politics, 154ff.
poverty program, xx, 86–87,
    140–141, 170–175
Powell, Adam Clayton, 157
"Power for Poor People," 51
power vs. love, 38
Prejudice and Your Child, 117
Price, Leontyne, 135
programs for civil rights, 141,
    164 170
Progress and Poverty, 172 173
property values, 124
Prothro, James W., 160
public housing, 210
    see also housing
Puerto Ricans, 141, 159
Pupil Placement decision, 11

Quakers, 82

race, 78
Race: Science and Politics, 73–74
racism, 12, 14, 49, 59, 71ff., 125–
    127, 137, 161–162, 183

*Racism and the Christian
    Understanding of Man,*
    73
Ramparts magazine, 3
Randolph, A. Philip, 39, 151,
    209
real estate values, 124
Red China, 198, 200
Reeb, James, 34
Reeb, Mrs. James, 34
religion, 77, 79, 102, 105, 132,
    133, 157, 190–191
rents, 122–123
Republican Party, 155
Reuther, Walter, 150
Ricks, Willie, 29
Riessman, Frank, 209
Rilleux, Norbert, 43
Robinson, Frank, 135
Robinson, Jackie, 135
Roget's Thesaurus, 42
Roosevelt, Eleanor, 157
Russell, Bill, 135
Rustin, Bayard, 120

school desegregation, 10, 11, 13,
    36, 57, 85
    see also integration *and*
    segregation
schools, *see* education
SCLC, xi, xii, 18, 23, 25, 29, 32,
    100, 151, 152–153
segregation, 13–14, 15, 17,
    101–107, 212–213
    see also desegregation,
    integration, *and* school
    desegregation
selfhood, 41, 44
    see also manhood

Sellers, Cleveland, 24–25
Selma, Ala., x, 1, 2, 3, 4, 5, 36,
    45, 52, 60, 166
semantics, 42
Sibelius, Jean, 135
sit-in movements, 36, 59
slave breeding, 112
slavery, 16, 39–44, 71ff., 110–
    116, 122, 125, 126, 127, 165
slums, *see* ghettos
SNCC, xi, 24–25, 26–28, 29,
    32, 49–50
Social Register, 212
somebodyness, 130–131
South Africa, 58
Southern Christian Leadership
    Conference, *see* SCLC
Southern freedom movement,
    ix, xii
Southern Rhodesia, 58
Soviet Union, 198
space exploration, 91
Stampp, Kenneth, 39
Statue of Liberty, 84
Stevenson, Adlai, 157
Stubbs, Bishop William, 78
Student Nonviolent
    Coordinating Committee,
    see SNCC
Sumner, Charles, 82
Supreme Court, 11

Tanganyika, 58
Teamsters Union, 150
tenant unions, 211–212
Teutonic Origins theory, 77–78,
    94
Thoreau, Henry David, 182
Tillich, Paul, 104
Tolstoy, Leo, 104

Toscanini, Arturo, 135
Toynbee, Arnold, 186
training, 205, 207–208
Turner, Nat, 58

Ulysses, 196
unemployment, 35
    see also employment
unions, 146–150, 159, 211–212
United Nations, 184, 195
United Shoe Machinery Co., 43
Urban Renewal Authority, 124

Van Winkle, Rip, 180–181
Vesey, Denmark, 58
Vietnam, xiv–xv, 7, 36, 92, 141,
    143
violence, 55ff., 90
    see also nonviolence
voter registration, 5–6
voting, 15, 160ff.
Voting Rights Act (1965), x, 1, 2,
    3, 35, 60, 85

Wagner Act, 212
Wallace, George G., 161
war, 90–91, 192, 193, 194–195
    see also Vietnam
war against poverty, *see* poverty
    program
Warren, Earl, 157
Washington, Booker T., 134, 137
Washington, George, 80–81, 181
Washington movement, 59
Washington Post, 91
Watts riot (1965), x, 2, 3, 21, 59,
    60, 120, 125
"We Shall Overcome," 26
welfare programs, 173–174
welfare unions, 211, 212

white backlash, xi, 2–3, 11,
  71 ff., 125–126
"white power," 50
white supremacy, 15, 77ff.,
  126–127, 161
Whitehead, Alfred North,
  179
Why We Can't Wait, 38
Williams, Daniel Hale, 43–44
Wirtz, W. Willard, 208
Wisconsin, University of, 78
Woods, Granville T., 43

"world house," 177ff.
Wretched of the Earth, The,
  56, 67–68
Wright, Richard, 29, 135
Wright brothers, 178

Yazoo City, Miss., 30
"Yes I Can," 135
Young, Andrew, 120
Young, Buddy, 135

Zambia, 58

THE KING LEGACY SERIES

In partnership with the Estate of Dr. Martin Luther King, Jr., Beacon Press is proud to share the great privilege and responsibility of furthering Dr. King's powerful message of peace, nonviolence, and social justice with a historic publishing program—the King Legacy.

The series will encompass Dr. King's most important writings, including sermons, orations, lectures, prayers, and all of his previously published books that are currently out of print. Published accessibly and in multiple formats, each volume will include new material from acclaimed scholars and activists, underscoring Dr. King's continued relevance for the twenty-first century and bringing his message to a new generation of readers.

thekinglegacy.org

Library of Congress Cataloging-in-Publication Data

King, Martin Luther, Jr., 1929–1968.
Where do we go from here : chaos or community? / Martin Luther King, Jr.
p.   cm.
Originally published: 1968.
Includes bibliographical references and index.
ISBN 978-0-8070-0076-2 (hardcover : alk. paper)
ISBN 978-0-8070-0067-0 (pbk. : alk. paper)
1. African Americans—History—1964– 2. African Americans—Civil rights.
3. Racism—United States. 4. United States—Race relations. I. Title.

E185.615.K5 2010   323.1196'073—dc22
2009035950